MAKING PEACE
WITH YOUR
THIGHS

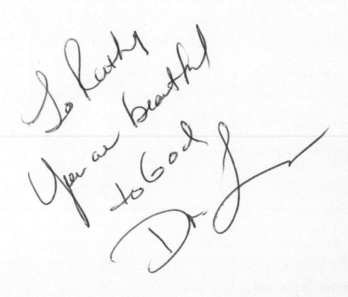

To Kathy
You are beautiful
to God
Dr.

MAKING PEACE
WITH YOUR
THIGHS

GET OFF THE SCALES
AND GET ON WITH YOUR LIFE

DR. LINDA MINTLE

INTEGRITY
PUBLISHERS®

Making Peace with Your Thighs

Published by Integrity Publishers, a division of Integrity Media, Inc., 660 Bakers Bridge Avenue, Suite 200, Franklin, TN 37067.

HELPING PEOPLE WORLDWIDE EXPERIENCE *the* MANIFEST PRESENCE *of* GOD.

This book is not intended to provide therapy, counseling, clinical advice, or treatment or to take the place of clinical advice and treatment from your personal physician or professional mental health provider. Readers are advised to consult their own qualified health-care physicians regarding mental health and medical issues. Neither the publisher nor the author takes any responsibility for any possible consequences from any treatment, action, or application of information in this book to the reader. Names, places, and identifying details have been changed to protect the privacy of individuals who may have similar experiences. The characters depicted here consist of composites of a number of people with similar issues, and the names and circumstances have been changed to protect their confidentiality. Any similarity between the names and stories of individuals described in this book to individuals known to readers is purely coincidental.

Cover Design: Wes Youssi
Cover Photo: Corbis
Interior Design: PerfecType, Nashville, TN

ISBN-13: 9-781-59145-426-7
ISBN-10: 1-59145-426-3

Printed in the United States of America

06 07 08 09 10 VG 9 8 7 6 5 4 3 2 1

To anyone who has ever felt less than who she was created to be.
And to my daughter, Katie, love your thighs and every other body part.
Remember, great things come in small packages!

Contents

Contents

Acknowledgments

I'd like to acknowledge my thighs. Still bumpy and filled with cellulite, they have been the inspiration for this book. Who knew? Without them and the angst they've caused through the years, I wouldn't be so personally invested in this subject. Add to this my red hair, freckles, albino skin, and a host of other body parts that have contributed to my writing!

To my longtime friend Jan, who gives me hope that it is possible to be a woman, accept your body, and not obsess. Of course, Jan, I have to thank your mom and dad (Marshall and Jean Jackson) for providing you with great genetic material and my family with great meals and entertainment.

To my brother, Dennis, for providing theology consults and keeping my computer working despite my attempts to crash my system. You saved me hours of headaches and rescued me from my computer-challenged self. Despite your incredibly busy schedule, you always took the time to help your sister.

Thanks to my husband, Norm—the other Dr. Mintle—for the new Aeron chair and flat-screen monitor. Both have helped with my long hours of sitting in front of the computer. My back and eyes would thank you except that I am encouraging women not to compartmentalize their body parts. My guess is you would like my entire body to thank you! Thanks for being one of the good guys.

To my children, Matt and Kaitlyn, who allow me to work for hours uninterrupted, knowing Dad doesn't miss a beat when Mom is preoccupied with work. And yes, maybe someday I'll write a book you'll actually want to read!

To my Integrity family who supports and encourages my writing, keep the laughter and great meals coming. To Byron, Joey, Kris, Rob, Scott, LaVenia, Barb, Betty, and Marie Prys, who jumped into the process fast and furious, and everyone else responsible for making peace with not only my thighs but each other, you are all greatly appreciated.

Finally, without faith, true peace isn't possible. No human effort can match what God can do when it comes to fully accepting and embracing who we are.

Imagine living your life free from distraction, distortion, obsession, and self-preoccupation. Imagine living in the moment and liberated from the patterns of the past while being excited about the future. Imagine accepting and even celebrating the body you've been given, knowing that one day it will be transformed into something more glorious than you could ever imagine.

Get off the Scales

Exhausted one night, I plopped down on the couch. With no husband in sight, it was my turn to engage in that familiar sport of channel surfing. As I clicked away searching for something worthwhile to watch, I was astounded at the number of shows about weight and body image. There was Kirstie Alley bouncing around the screen in *Fat Actress*. Waif-like Mary-Kate Olsen discussing her recent eating disorder treatment. Kate Moss looking scary-skinny. Commercials telling me to supersize it and have it my way. Graphic cosmetic surgery. Beyonce discussing her bootylicious image. And the Dove girls parading around in their underwear!

From fat to thin, thin to fat, the polarized media messages felt like cultural whiplash. *Be thin, but not too thin. Big is beautiful. Fat is a rejection of the undernourished look. Nip it, tuck it. You can't be too thin or too beautiful.* My head was spinning!

Even though the average American woman is a size twelve, to hear the TV tell it, size two is our goal, girls. But there's one problem I have with the fantasy. Have you seen a size two, or worse yet, a size *zero* pants? Next time you are at the Gap, pull a pair of size zero jeans off the rack and do what I did—try to fit your leg, just one leg, inside! It's impossible! Only my arm fits! It's enough to make any woman feel like a desperate housewife!

Let's face it, life as females is not easy when it comes to feeling good about our bodies. We are held hostage by mediated images—whether our position is CEO, housewife, supermodel, teacher, actress, or mom. And if you thought you were alone or suffering from some Hollywood-only disorder, think again.

Listen to women discuss their bodies in the checkout lines at the local Kroger. Ask any woman what it's like trying on bathing suits at the department store. Notice the effort involved in finding just the right pair of jeans that hide our physical flaws. And there is no question that body insecurity is found in the fly-over states as well as the right and left coasts. It's red and blue, and respects no one. With that said, let me be the first to welcome you to the sisterhood of the dissatisfied traveling pants!

Ladies, we are bonded together by body insecurities! Even admitting this makes me mad. I don't want to sound so superficial. After all, it's a new millennium—forty years past the feminist movement. I am supposed to believe my appearance doesn't define me, yet even though I know there is more to my inner life than the food I put in my stomach, more to my outer appearance than the clothes I wear, I struggle to accept my body as it is. And I know I can always benefit from that extra five-pound weight loss.

I'm not alone. Weight obsession and physical fitness are national pastimes. Witness the popularity of makeover and plastic surgery television programs and the billions of dollars spent on diet and exercise products. Turn on your television set and watch twenty-five women abandon their brains to seduce one bachelor using only their physical beauty and sex appeal. None of them are even close to being a few pounds overweight. No, these women are all thin, stunning, and ready to display their worked-out bodies in bathing suits.

Or watch gorgeous and thin *Desperate Housewives'* Teri Hatcher tell interviewer Diane Sawyer she has been insecure all her life and is just now beginning to feel not so flawed. I'm trying to be empathetic, Teri, really I am; I'm just not quite there yet.

And neither are most of us. We long to accept our bodies as they are. Yet the line between reality and fantasy is often blurred and reminds me of a story. I have a friend named Bill who was a comedian. His wife, Sally, was a high school principal. When Bill was doing stand-up comedy, his life was lived mostly on the road. Such is the life of a comic.

Whenever my husband and I would get together with Sally and our mutual friend Barbara, Bill was always in Toledo, Kansas City, Atlanta, or some other city doing stand-up. Because we never saw Bill, we all began to wonder if he and Sally were really married. They claimed they were, and they had wedding pictures and terrific wedding stories, but we rarely saw the two of them together because of their schedules.

The joke became that Bill was "mythical." He didn't really exist; we just made him up because Sally liked the idea of being married. From that point on, we referred to him as "Mythical Bill." Eventually, Mythical Bill gave up his traveling comedy gigs and decided that Sally was worth seeing more often. He turned the myth into reality.

When it comes to our bodies, we need to turn myth into reality. The perfectly sculpted body doesn't really exist, but we like to pretend it does. Though we haven't seen it in the natural, others testify it is indeed real. We are told that with the right efforts, we can attain it, *if* we:

- exercise four to five hours a day with a personal trainer.
- hire a personal chef to cook healthy food and prepare all our meals and snacks.

- consult with fashion experts whose designer friends are dying for us to wear their clothes as advertisements.
- have tons of money to buy the multitude of available self-care products.
- hire professional makeup and hair artists and only be photographed in perfect light.

Only then may our bodies in some way resemble that mythical, perfectly sculpted body.

And that body is everywhere, isn't it? Plastered on billboards, splashed on the pages of magazines, moving and jiggling on movie screens. Yet we forget how that perfectly sculpted body is computer-altered and airbrushed. In our heads, we know professional makeup, hair stylists, fashion experts, and lighting make all the difference in the world. But we still think these women are real and represent what we are supposed to look like!

When the myth *seems* like reality—when we see "perfect looking" women on the subway or walking in the mall—we never think they could dislike their bodies as much as we do. Chances are, they do. We can't envision the cellulite on their thighs or the stomach roll carefully camouflaged by fashion, but it's probably there.

Because we are exposed daily to images of mythical goddesses we are supposed to look like but fall short of, we tend to think everyone should be beautiful, well-manicured, and thin. Our standards of beauty have become incredibly narrow. And while less than 5 percent of us can actually achieve this supermodel look, this doesn't stop us from trying.[1]

The impact of the idealized body myth became reality for me one day as I was sitting in a women's study group. The topic of conversation turned to teasing. One by one the women recalled painful memories of childhood teasing related to their bodies.

One woman who had a beautiful upturned nose hated fifth grade because her classmates regularly made fun of that feature. Another remembered the pain of being overweight and teased. Tears streamed down her face as she spoke. She still saw herself as that overweight child who wanted to hide from the world. And my own crazy body thoughts resurfaced in my mind as we talked.

I wasn't surprised by the discussion of these early hurts and rejections—we all have a story or two. But I was surprised by the power they still held. It was as if each woman reverted to the age of the hurt and relived the moment like it happened yesterday. And I thought, *What is missing that we can't seem to get past this? And why have we allowed such narrow definitions of beauty to define us?*

The purpose of this book is to help us regain something important that has been lost. Too often we allow ourselves to be defined by our imperfect parts. We need to experience wholeness again . . . or maybe for the first time. We achieve this by defying the body myths and living in a new reality. This new reality includes all three parts of our being—body, soul, and spirit. When we surrender our spirit to God, we can renew our minds, free our emotions, and accept the bodies we have been given.

As we learn to resist cultural prescriptions of the feminine ideal and embrace our uniqueness, we can create a new space— a friendlier inner environment in which to live. One that empha- sizes grace, not judgment. One that has the strength to overcome negative thoughts and anxious feelings. One that provides hope and not despair. For most of us, this will require a reclaiming of our bodies. We will have to question our motivations, our obses- sions, and our constant need to improve on our looks. Most of all, we will need to recognize the spirit within us that gives life to our mortal bodies.

The fact is, we have only one body to work with while here

on Earth. We can dislike it and obsess over it, or we can use that time and energy to develop other parts of ourselves and bring wholeness back to our lives. We can blame our dads, fault our mothers, point to that insensitive schoolmate, or complain about *The Bachelor* for our insecurities. Basically, we can remain victims of our own crazy thinking and the crazy thinking of others. Or we can rethink our lives and make new choices. Choices that will lead to an acceptance of our one-of-a-kind design and bring new contentment.

I write from my perspective as a Caucasian woman influenced by the larger culture yet with my own unique experiences. I believe my story is typical. I grew up with a multitude of insecurities and rarely felt attractive. I had trouble accepting the body I was given. My personal struggle originated both from my own mind and from outside influences. As I share parts of my life and the professional knowledge I have, my hope is that you will come alongside of me as a sister and learn to appreciate your body as well.

I'm convinced there will always be a longing to break out of the physical boundaries of our bodies. That longing is deep within us and prompts us to want something more . . . something that can't be satisfied by commercial solutions. Yet a deeper transformation must take place—one that renews our minds and calms our souls from body obsession. For now, our bodies are our homes, our spiritual temples. They are to be cherished and respected. Care for them and keep them as healthy as possible. And in doing so, let's resist the myths, change our attitudes along with our culture, and together, make peace with our thighs!

PART ONE

Lessons in
Basic Anatomy

CHAPTER 1

Thighs and Sighs of the Times

Every morning after my shower, I stared at my body in the full-length mirror. I was a teenager in junior high school, and I felt awkward.

Spending time in front of a mirror is typical teenage behavior. What wasn't typical was what I noticed on my right thigh one day. There, positioned like the Rock of Gibraltar, was this "massive" bump. I didn't know when it appeared or how it had formed. It just . . . was there.

Like a small volcano on the side of my thigh, the bump was visually distracting. So much so that no matter what I put on, it created fashion havoc. There was simply no way to adjust my pants to make both of the legs fall normally to the floor.

I was puzzled. At 5'5" and 120 pounds, I wasn't overweight. Though not thrilled about my red hair, freckles, and albino skin, the rest of my body seemed to at least be in proportion. My breasts were full, my waist slim, and my hips appropriately curvy. But under the wide belt of my hip-huggers was the thing that made me different from all those girls in my class. Of course, I only compared myself to the perfect, popular girls, but to me, "the bump" was like a massive pimple on my nose. You just could not miss it. All my attention—and everyone else's, I was sure—was focused on my lopsided thigh.

I made several futile attempts to hide the bump, but the fashion world was unkind. Hip-hugging pants (the precursor to low-rise jeans) just accentuated my imperfections. Tops and T-shirts were short and could not be pulled over the problem spot. So, I resorted to my own solutions. I pounded the bump—hitting it with my fist to try and flatten it. It didn't budge. One of my friends suggested taking a rolling pin to my thigh to force the bump into the proper shape! Although this felt good, it never made a dent on the problem. And it didn't seem to matter how active I was, the stubborn bump stood its ground.

Frustrated and worried, I wondered if it was time to seek professional help, because my fears were getting the best of me. Maybe it was a genetic deformity. Or a tumor. Or caused by wearing tight pants. Or maybe a part of my thigh grew too fast and was waiting for the rest of my body to catch up. What if I needed injections? What if my doctor wanted to cut the bump off?

My anxiety was building. I needed help. I decided that at my next pediatric checkup, I would muster my courage and confront my fears. My pediatrician would know the cause and solution. No matter how bad the news might be, I reasoned, I could handle it now that I was more mature. If I had a tumor growing on my thigh, I needed to face reality. The bump sure looked like a tumor to me. Of course, I had never seen a tumor, but I imagined this was what it must look like.

The day I walked into Dr. Elghammer's office, I was nervous. He began the exam. "Linda, do you have any questions?" It was now or never. My heart began to pound. My palms were sweaty. It was time—I needed to know my fate.

"Yes," I nervously answered. "I have this bump on my thigh. It has me very worried. You should look at it. Whatever it is, I can handle it."

Dr. Elghammer became very serious. *Oh no, this can't be good,* I thought to myself. Slowly, I lifted my gown and showed him the site of concern.

"I'm wondering if it's a tumor or something." I tried to sound nonchalant, but I was bracing for the worst.

He soberly stared at the mass, and in my mind, the expression on his face said it all. Something was dreadfully wrong. It was a tumor and I was going to die.

I'm too young to die; I don't want to die. I took a deep breath and waited for him to answer.

Then, in a moment, my world changed. A big smile came across his face. He carefully covered up my thigh and looked me in the eye with a reassuring smile.

"This is nothing to be concerned about. It's not a tumor."

Well, then what is it?" I replied, relieved but still wondering.

"It's a fat deposit called cellulite."

"What does that mean?"

"It means you have a deposit of fat on your right thigh."

"What? No, I don't. Why is it there? How did it get there? I mean, why would fat settle on my right thigh? I'm only a kid."

Dr. Elghammer continued. "Sometimes fat deposits just appear on different parts of our bodies—on our arms, legs, waist, etc. You just happen to have one on your right thigh."

"Well, that's just not right. I don't want a fat deposit on my thigh. It looks bad . . . all crinkly and ugly when I put on my bathing suit. How do I make it go away?"

"You don't," he said. (These were the days before liposuction.)

"And I can't tell you why the fat decided to deposit there. But it did. It's not a problem. It's harmless."

Easy for you to say, I thought to myself. *You don't wear hip-huggers or have to be seen by your girlfriends in a bathing suit when you go to the beach. You aren't 14 with red hair and freckles that already make you different.*

My next reaction was to be mortified—all my worry and concern was over a *fat deposit* I had to just live with and accept.

Thus went my incredible introduction to cellulite. The enemy of body acceptance now had a name.

I needed revelation.

I needed therapy.

I needed help. But all I could do was sigh and look at my thigh.

It's all in the viewing

Body image is no more than a mental picture we hold of ourselves. And that mental picture can be positive, negative, or somewhere in-between. Body image develops through our perceptions but also involves our attitudes, imaginations, emotions, and physical feelings, as well as the accumulation of others' comments about us and their own view of themselves.

The problem with body image is that it's usually based on our overall feelings about ourselves, and these feelings can't always be trusted and are not necessarily based in reality. Let's think a minute about this. When our perceptions are negative, a small bump becomes the Washington Monument. Upset, dislike, even hatred of our bodies can result. In my case, I didn't hate my thighs, but I sure did dislike them. I would have happily traded them for someone else's. "Yes, I'll take the Cindy Crawford thighs, please."

The good news is that both our body image—and those feelings—are changeable. We don't have to fall victim to our feelings or distorted ideas. We can be free to accept what we've been given and make the best of it.

Our goal is to learn to accept our God-given bodies and even get to the point of celebrating them. Now I realize that for most of us, acceptance and celebration remain an act of faith at this point. That's OK. It took me a long time to get there too. And honestly, I still have my moments. But it did help me to understand that we don't inherit this propensity to negatively evaluate what we see in the mirror—at least not genetically. There wasn't a "dislike your thighs" gene that was passed down to me through the generations. Of course, the thigh gene itself *was* inherited, and there is nothing short of liposuction I can do about it, but the like or dislike of my thighs was learned on my own along with a little help from others and the culture.

In fact, no one ever has to point out our flaws for us to have a distorted body image. Have you ever noticed that? I don't remember one single person ever commenting on my thighs—positive or negative. The fact is, we are really good at seeing our own physical flaws. we don't need training for this. You might even say we are experts: we constantly make comparisons with those whom we deem are better than us. The end result is frustration, dissatisfaction, or anxiety about our physical appearance.

In my case, I viewed the bump as not only something that made me unattractive, but a fault that made me less valuable than the girls around me. Really, though, the bump did not equal "unattractive" until I allowed it to mean just that. Rather than figuring out why I gave this small bump so much power in my life, I preferred to concentrate my energies on improving my appearance. And that strategy continued into adult life. However, it was not a strategy that served me well; I needed a spiritual awakening, but that came later.

Naked and not loving it

For years I've worked with people who suffer from extreme body distortion problems, usually due to eating disorders or abuse. Yet every healthy woman I know also struggles to fully accept her body. Because of this, I've wondered if it is even possible to see ourselves without distortion.

What I do know is this: it is difficult to correct our distorted body image apart from a spiritual lens and an appreciation for our spiritual history. (More on the history in a moment.) Without a spiritual perspective, we fail to understand that what we see in the mirror is not the whole picture. As the apostle Paul reminds us, "We don't yet see things clearly. We're squinting in a fog, peering through a mist. But it won't be long before the weather clears and the sun shines bright! We'll see it all then, see it all as clearly as God sees us, knowing him directly just as he knows us!"[1]

Right now, we don't have that complete 20/20 view. So we may try to improve the imperfections with items like Botox or cellulite creams. Yet that doesn't change what we see. In an attempt to privately cope with our insecurities, we may avoid the mirror and pretend we don't care. Others of us have moments of acceptance but continue to fight feelings of inadequacy and insecurity. And some of us just downright hate our bodies and can't free ourselves from the emotional pain. But living at any of these points still means that we are, in some way, stuck.

Wherever we fall on the body acceptance continuum, we need someone bigger than ourselves to give us proper perspective, to help us remove the distortions, and to rid us of our inadequate feelings. Then we'll be able to get off the scale, get away from the mirror, get out of the plastic surgeon's office, and get on with our lives.

For years, I searched for something inside myself that could pull me out of the tendency to feel inadequate or need to do better. I believed in self-determination. *Try this. Do that. Buy this. Pull yourself up by the bootstraps. If you don't like it, change it.* None of this helped long-term. I also noticed that when I worked with women who had extreme body image distortions attached to their eating disorders, the eating disorders might improve with professional therapy, but their poor body image lingered.

Feminists say hatred of the body stems from culture's oppression and manipulation of women. This may be true, but it isn't the full picture.

I now understand that the spiritual history I share with the first woman is part of the root problem that must be addressed. Transformation only comes when the *full* story is discovered, for while there is no body image gene to inherit, there is a spiritual heritage that must be traced if we ever want to come to terms with our bodies.

This spiritual heritage requires us to believe in a Creator. If we believe we were an accident or a result of fate, we have no moorings on which to ground our thinking and no meaning to guide our lives. As Rick Warren so aptly reminds us in *The Purpose Driven® Life*, we all are created with a purpose, and it is bigger than our personal fulfillment. There has to be an overarching story that impacts ours in order for our lives to make sense and be transformed. Let's take a look at where it all began so we can understand where we're going.

In the beginning

Body image distortion began in the beginning. In the third chapter of the book of Genesis in the Bible, an explanation of how we moved from originally accepting our created bodies to embracing feelings of shame and inadequacy is provided. In the short form, and to put it bluntly, the origins of our distorted body image developed when a man and woman decided to share a treat. Didn't you just know food had to be involved in this? The only surprise is that the food was fruit, not chocolate!

In the beginning, God created Adam and Eve in His own image. They were flawless, unaffected by sin. And the Lord of the universe gave them His seal of approval by calling them—and the rest of His creation—"good." Picture it: Two perfect bodies roamed the garden—naked and unashamed—and one of those bodies belonged to a woman! I bet Eve loved her thighs and Adam adored them. Body acceptance was at an all-time high.

Most of us know the rest of the account. God tells Adam that the two can eat from any tree in the garden except for the tree of the knowledge of good and evil. That tree was forbidden, with the added instruction that if they ate from that tree, they would die. Now, I can't imagine any food being worth that price, but apparently Eve felt differently. Maybe it was a tree of dark chocolate-covered strawberries with Starbucks dripping for sap!

Anyway, the serpent comes to Eve and asks her if God really said what He said. She basically says yes and adds that touching the fruit is a no-no as well. Then the serpent lies to her and says, "You won't die. In fact, you'll be like God, knowing good and evil."

The next part of Eve's temptation relates to our discussion. It involved seduction in three areas:

- personal benefit
- focus on appearance
- false wisdom

When Eve saw that the fruit on the forbidden tree was "good for food," she was enticed. Never mind that God said to avoid it; she saw a personal benefit here. It looked like it would taste great and provide nourishment.

When we are deceived, we make certain choices solely because we believe there is personal gain involved. Attaining the perfect body usually includes this temptation. We're convinced there is real benefit to all the obsessing we do and all the improvements we make. Our culture reinforces this. Beauty, thinness, big breasts, and whatever else equal success, opportunity, men, even money. We are drawn in by the potential for personal reward. Especially when the benefit to us would be instant and, we think, permanent!

Eve also noticed that the fruit was pleasing to the eye. She took her attention off of God and the truth of what He'd said, and got all caught up in appearances. How often does this happen to us? We get wind of something that falsely promises us incredible physical results, and we want it. Offers of plastic surgery, youthful creams, and other beauty aids are so tempting because they are "guaranteed" to boost our appearance—to make us more pleasing to the eye. But like Eve, when we turn impulsive and care too much about how things look, we lose sight of the long-term consequences of deception. Those consequences cause havoc in our lives.

Finally, Eve believed she could behave independently of God and be OK. For that moment, she didn't trust what God had said was true; she did her own thing—followed her own solution . . . and something shifted. In fact, everything changed.

Now, there is no indication that sin changed their physical bodies outright. Adam and Eve still had those glorious, perfected forms. What did change, however, was their *awareness* or perceptions. After eating from the forbidden tree, Adam's and Eve's eyes were opened. They didn't become like God as the serpent promised, but they did become aware of their nakedness. And apparently they didn't like what they saw because they tried to hide their bodies.

Think about that. Even people with perfect bodies wanted to cover up and hide! Their perceptions became distorted, even though they were still outwardly beautiful. Separated from God, they felt exposed. The result was shame. When sin entered, their spirits died. Shame and sin took over where once there was goodness and satisfaction and delight. Their perceptions of one another shifted, as well as their views of themselves. Everything was now distorted.

The flashing neon sign here is that perfect bodies don't fix the problem!

Now I like the next part of the story because it helps me see how normal it is to be a slow learner who, if not careful, continues to make a mess out of her life. Adam's and Eve's newfound awareness led them to once again take matters into their own hands . . . this time by clothing themselves. Don't you just want to shout at them and say, "Quit while you're ahead!"

Do you see the problem? Every time Adam and Eve made a decision apart from God, they got in trouble. Their solution this time was to quickly sew together the first designer fig-leaf outfits and cover themselves. But because it's impossible to hide from God, God found Adam and asked him a question, "Who told you that you were naked?"

God knows the answer. He's God. So why would He ask such a question? Could it be that He was making a point? He's not upset by their nakedness; He designed those incredible bodies and declared them good, remember? Rather, God is asking a question related to their hiding and feelings of shame.

When God asked where Adam was, he responded to God's question by saying that he hid because he was afraid and naked. But like the messed up people we are, Adam goes on to blame Eve and God by saying that the woman he was given was the problem. And then when God asks Eve what happened, she blames the serpent. Blame is everywhere. No one is acknowledging that they made mistakes and need help.

Adam's and Eve's view of their nakedness changed based on their decisions to act independently from God. Eve believed the lie and sinned. Adam ignored God's voice of authority and sinned. Sin resulted in fear and hiding and a condemnation of their natural state. Adam's and Eve's newfound knowledge of good and evil brought them anxiety in their naked identity. On their own, they tried to cover their nakedness and not feel shame, but they failed. And self-hatred began.

To me, this story explains, in part, why we struggle so much in the area of complete body acceptance. Our perceptions are distorted. Like Eve, we tend to listen to the voices all around us who don't have our best interests in mind. When we take matters into our own hands and try to deal with those perceptions without God, shame keeps us buying more products, taking unhealthy supplements to lose weight, going under the knife for risky surgery, and more. Did you ever think about that? It's shame that motivates us, not excitement! Do we really want to keep living like that? Shame also distorts the image in the mirror and says to us, "You are inadequate and don't measure up."

The good news is that God sees us in our natural state, naked and all, and He doesn't shame us. He intentionally formed us just as we are . . . for a unique purpose! It's when we attempt to separate ourselves from Him—to live life on our own terms and according to the images of this world—that we start to feel shame and dislike our bodies.

When we try to deal with distorted images of ourselves apart from God, we won't be successful. Our self-deception is just too strong. Thankfully, God pursued Adam and Eve in their naked state. He didn't hide from them but pursued them. I love that about God. We are the ones in hiding, not Him. When Adam and Eve were ashamed, they really needed God to take control. Someone bigger had to intervene. And that's just what happened.

God had them discard the fig leaves and made tunics of animal skin to clothe them. This is important not because it was a fashion shift, but because of the significance of God clothing them instead of them clothing themselves.

When God clothed Adam and Eve, it wasn't because of shame. It was a covering of protection. Forget the ineffective fig leaves. They were the first man's and woman's attempt to solve their shame problem on their own.

Skins, though, had significance. They required the shedding of blood. God offered the first blood sacrifice to save Adam and Eve from spiritual death. What an incredible provision and foreshadowing of our need for a personal Savior who would keep us from destroying ourselves and give us an alternative to solving our problems on our own.

Just as was true for the first humans, our Designer is capable of covering our distorted perceptions with truth. He does not condemn us or our bodies. He offers grace and love.

Dealing with our perceptions requires a reality beyond ourselves and others. Will we listen to our own or others' thoughts, and will we act accordingly? Or will we listen to God—the One who formed us in the womb and called us by name before we were born—and believe what He says? The path we choose will determine how well we come to accept our bodies.

The first step in achieving body acceptance is to acknowledge our nakedness, our neediness, before God. Second, we must decide what will be allowed to "cover" us—our own efforts, the words of family members, cultural images, procedures by plastic surgeons. All these can keep us in hiding with feelings of shame and insecurity. Wouldn't you rather let God's truth speak to you? Wouldn't you prefer to listen when He calls you beautiful and tells you why?

Personally, I don't want to cover myself with fig leaves any longer. I don't sew anyway. That's not to say I haven't tried to make my own coverings, but this hasn't worked. I still felt naked. It was only when I allowed God to clothe me in His truth that I could stand before Him, just as I am, and experience no shame.

Sisters, it's time to hand over the fig leaves and let God sew us garments that protect us from the deceiving voices in our heads. We have a spiritual heritage that brings truth to our body, soul, and spirit. It's our choice: to stand alone, naked and ashamed, or, with God's help, to make peace with our thighs . . . and all our other body parts.

The Lessons

- Things that go bump in the night may not be so scary.
- Distortion is part of our spiritual history.
- When our designer is God, we are clothed in truth.

CHAPTER 2

The Hair Is Always Blonder
on the Other Side

I was born a redhead, and it's drawn lots of unwanted attention over the years. Especially from grandmas. They would pat me on the head and marvel at the color—even stop my mom on the street to talk about it. Of course, I was taught to be polite and thank them for the compliments, but inside I was worried. If grandmas like moth balls, doilies, and babushkas, it couldn't be good that they liked my red hair!

Some people would have liked all that attention, but I didn't. My brother Denny terrorized me about my hair by saying things like, "I'd rather be dead than red on the head." On one level, I agreed with him. My hair was too bright for my very white face and stood out too much. I looked like a Campbell's tomato soup can—red on the top, white on the bottom. Tasty but not tasteful! Nevertheless, I learned how to get even with Denny.

Because he was the "spiritually sensitive" child of our family

(I know that "terrorizing" and "spiritually sensitive" don't sound like they go together, but he had the capacity for both), I found his weakness and played on it. He had this secret fear that he wouldn't make it into heaven. As a result, every night before Denny went to bed, he would ask me to forgive him for teasing me. I soon learned that if I said no to his request, I could torture him with thoughts of being left behind should Jesus return. Because we were theologically confused, this worked like a charm. (And I'm happy to report that his spiritually sensitive heart eventually won out over his tortuous side. Today he is the Reverend Denny!)

In any case, I was certain that if I had been born blonde like Denny, or brunette like my other brother, Gary, fewer people would have patted my head and life would have been easier.

By the time I was in high school, my red hair wasn't just the enemy—blondes in general had become the bane of my existence. My blonde envy and I were painfully aware that redheaded science freaks with freckles and albino skin were not the popular girls. It was the star cheerleader, the prom queen, and their friends—the blonde-haired, blue-eyed girls who looked like they'd stepped out of a *Glamour* magazine. They were in every way the chosen ones. And they certainly didn't like science.

Adding salt to the wound were the yearbook entries I'd read at the end of each school year that fellow students had signed for the blondies. "To a really cool girl who is so fun." "I'm so glad to be your friend. Let's get together over the summer." "To a cute girl who all the boys adore."

My yearbook entries read . . . well, differently: "To the only girl I know who can go to Florida and get her hair sunburned." Or "To the girl whose hair gets rusty in the rain." And there was an overabundance of signings wishing me good luck with the boys. Did I need extra help? Redheads were definitely the minority and different, and in high school, I didn't want to be different. I wanted to have more fun like all the blondes were having.

I thought about dyeing my hair blonde, but it would have been so obvious it was fake. My albino skin—which didn't tan but just sort of broke out in red splotches—and freckles would be a dead giveaway. And there were no creams or sprays back then to fake a tan. These were ancient days before even the advent of tanning beds (not that I am recommending them). So living in a beach town like I was, I felt doomed by my "dreadful" locks.

And yet, there was a lone voice urging me to hair acceptance. It came in a yearbook entry from fellow student Mitzi Knauf, a cute little blonde who wrote, "I hope your hair color doesn't change with the years, because I can't imagine you without it." God bless Mitzi Knauf wherever she is today. She gave me hope.

Unfortunately, her encouragement wasn't enough to end my envy. At college, where I met my future husband, Norm, I made a mistake one night that nearly sealed for all time my belief that redheads were deadheads. On that fateful evening, he and I were sitting out on the lawn in front of one of the dorms. For some reason, I decided to ask him what his ideal woman would look like. We were nothing more than friends at the time, but I was hoping our relationship would progress beyond friendship, so I *really* don't know what possessed me to ask him such a ridiculous thing! Maybe because I was a psychology major, I thought these insight-type questions would help me get to know him better. Unfortunately, I only had one psychology course under my belt at that time and didn't realize I was setting him up to disappoint me.

Since we were just friends, he felt very comfortable and answered my no-win question without hesitation: "Oh, that's easy. She would be petite and brunette with dark eyes." Relieved that the woman of his dreams wasn't blonde, I sighed for a moment. Then I realized Norm wasn't describing me! I became frantic inside, sure that he would never find me attractive. Amazingly, he did, but for years I never believed him. I tortured my poor husband *ad nauseam* with my insecurities, thinking he married down in the attractiveness department—all because of a single stupid question asked years prior. Talk about regrets for both of us! So here's a piece of advice from that experience: Ladies, don't ask such ridiculous questions; and guys, don't answer them.

Life, literature, and art only seemed to confirm my observations. With the exception of perhaps redhead Nicole Kidman, Americans prefer blondes, and I was not one of them. Witness the Miss America Pageant. How many redheads make it to the finals? None. How many blondes in white dresses do? I don't have that many fingers and toes! A few years ago, a redhead actually did make it to the top 10! But of course she ultimately lost to . . . you guessed it—a blonde in a white dress!

My literary hero in grade school was Pippi Longstocking, the fearless nine-year-old redhead who lived all alone in a tiny little town. Pippi was known for two things: her incredible physical strength (she could've taken down my two older brothers) and her carrot-colored hair braided so tight the braids stuck straight out of her head. However, she was not only a fictional character, but I would now diagnose her with a serious case of ADHD. So much for redheaded role models.

Great art has it in for redheads too. In Marion Roach's book, *Roots of Desire: The Myth, Meaning and Sexual Power of Red Hair*, she points out that the ceiling of the Sistine Chapel has a blonde, innocent, pre-apple Eve painted on it. But as your eye finds the scene of Eve being kicked out of the Garden of Eden, she is naked with nothing but long *red* hair draping her body. Her transformation from purity to sinner involves a change in hair color!

Then if you travel to St. Paul's Cathedral in London, you will

notice a similar transformation in the mosaics. Once Eve suc-
cumbs to temptation, her hair becomes blood red and mankind
suffers. No wonder redheads are accused of being hotheaded—
we've been blamed for the sins of humanity for thousands of
years!

And since we are mentioning sins, another infamous sinner
has red hair in historical paintings. Judas, who betrayed Jesus, has
been repeatedly painted with fiery locks!

And here is a newfound fact that is frightening: a study at the
University of Louisville found that redheaded women need 20
percent more anesthesia to be sedated properly for surgery than
other people![1] Fortunately, I learned this *after* having a number
of surgeries! I'll have to add this information to my wallet like
one of those cards for diabetics. "Attention all surgeons: Check
my purse and hair color before proceeding."

My ramblings may sound superficial, but they are the
thoughts of a young adult trying to like her body while her peers
and the culture are busy trying to define what is beautiful for her.
It's funny how such perceptions stay with a person when not
addressed or corrected. And yet many of us don't. We live our
lives with these secret struggles . . . trying to love the bodies we've
been given but hating them or wanting desperately to change
them.

With a little maturity under my belt, you'll be glad to know I
adjusted enough to being a redhead that I decided perhaps just a
touch of blonde—strawberry blonde highlights, to be exact—was
the way to go. I tried this and liked it, but I could never bring
myself to completely dye my hair blonde because of those penned
words from Mitzi Knauf, and because it just wouldn't be me. All
my life I'd been known as the girl with the red hair. Becoming all
blonde would be like trying to change nationalities—obvious and
unnatural. So I struggled along. Somewhere in my thirties, I

started liking my red hair. I suspect it had less to do with the color of my hair and more to do with becoming comfortable in the body God gave me. I had transitioned from anxiety and discontentment to acceptance, but what caused it?

For me, it was a tiny baby I held in my arms. He was the most beautiful baby I had ever seen, and he was mine. When sunlight danced over his little round head, shocks of red could be seen running through his hair. I would look at him and marvel, "Only God could create a baby this beautiful, this precious, and this perfect." *Perfect*. I saw him as perfect, and suddenly I knew how God saw me. Not a mistake, not a blonde in waiting, but the very *red* apple of his eye. I got the message then: the way He colored my hair was perfect.

I thought about my mom and the tiny baby she'd held in her arms decades before. *She must have thought the same thing about me.* I remembered all the times she told me how special my hair was and how I would later come to realize it was beautiful because it was the hair God gave me. Without it, she said, I wouldn't be me. (Sounds like Mitzi Knauf again.) Like my mom, God was able to see something I couldn't—a beauty He had designed! My red hair was part of how I was wonderfully and fearfully made. In the past, I had only focused on the fearful part.

Perhaps the baby Jesus had shocks of red in His hair. OK, that's a stretch, but I bet Mary didn't look at him and think, *You know, I wish he was blond.* No, I'm sure Mary looked at the tiny babe like I looked at my infant son and thought, *He's perfect, beautiful, precious.* The color of his hair was irrelevant. She was holding her baby boy.

When we are different—when we don't fit the media stereotype or our peer group's idea of popular—we often come to see ourselves as less attractive, never considering that maybe our parents saw us as beautiful beings created miraculously by God. And we forget to consult our heavenly Father for His opinion. Yet He is the one who, before we were formed in our mother's womb, decided the DNA of our hair—red, black, brown, blonde; stringy, thick, curly, straight, thin.

The irony of life is this: now that I've embraced my red hair as a blessing that makes me special, I'm morphing into a blonde. That's right, today my hair looks blonder then ever! With age, the red is fading, and you know what? I miss it. It is my defining feature. Adored by older women, made fun of by the young, seen as a bit exotic by adults, my red hair is me.

For someone who lived half her life thinking the hair was always blonder on the other side, it's good to know I've made peace with what I've been given. And I know it's true because finally, Mitzi Knauf, I can agree . . . I can't imagine me without my red hair either!

The Lessons

- Do not covet your neighbor's hair.
- You wouldn't be you without it.

CHAPTER 3

Led by the Nose

Whose nose do you really like? If I took a survey and asked this question, would any of us answer, "My own?" OK, I'll take a survey. Raise your hand if your nose is your favorite nose. I don't see any hands. Well, maybe one or two of you raised your hands, but rhinoplasties don't count!

My nose became an issue for me in junior high. (Are you beginning to see a pattern here? Body awareness and junior high!) The small bump in the middle and the size of my nose on my petite face seemed to be all wrong. What was God thinking? Surely He must have blinked while He was finishing my DNA package. Or perhaps He was distracted and put the nose of someone else on me instead.

Think about it. If God was multitasking (definitely His feminine side) during my creation and had to attend to a more pressing matter like world peace, my nose could well have taken a back seat for that critical moment. And since God doesn't make mistakes, He probably took a quick look and said to Himself,

"Ahh, this nose will build character. I think I'll go with it." *Voila, le nez!*

However it happened, as a teenager I was convinced that my nose was the thing that kept me from being attractive. And since there simply wasn't much you could do about your physical features back in my day—you got what you got—I had to accept what I'd been given.

That acceptance process took more than a few years, but I was resourceful enough to never be without a strategy. My first plan was the culmination of hours of staring at my nose in the mirror and trying to decide my best angle. Did my nose look better straight-on, to the right, with my head tilted a bit to the left? Yes, it probably was an exercise in futility, since I couldn't walk around holding my head in one position all the time, but I always felt better when I pretended to take charge of my life.

After careful study, I decided straight-on was best. I would avoid letting people see me in profile. In school, this meant I had to sit *behind* cute guys so that when they'd turn around to ask me a question or pass me a paper, they'd be looking at my face from the front. The second part of my strategy was to wow them with personality. I figured if I did this, they wouldn't even notice my nose. This took some doing—I had to be funny, entertaining, and the life of the class. Finally, my master plan required me to become physically agile. Do you know how difficult it is trying to outrun everyone in your class to secure the desk behind a guy you are trying to impress? Timing is everything.

Here's how it works. You have to be the first person to the classroom. Then you linger at the door, pretending to do something important. You watch and wait for the cute guy to select a desk. Here's the tricky part. Once he chooses a seat, you have to make a mad dash to the desk behind him. But if, let's say, one of the popular girls tries to sit behind the targeted guy, you have to casually intercept her, slide into the chair, put a big smile on your face, and say, "Oh, I'm sorry. Did you want to sit here?" They rarely say yes. They just look at you with disgust and move on.

Most of the time I could manage this intricately timed dash, although occasionally I found myself pushed aside or chided by an entitled cheerleader. But by the second quarter of the year, the stress of it all got to me. It was exhausting trying to be the first one to class every day, and it took too much mental energy to secure the right seat each time.

Although my sprinting skills would have won me a spot on the track team, I needed a new plan for high school. The halls were too long, the classes too far away. I would be lucky to make it to class on time, so there was no way I was going to beat any-one to a specific seat. One day the light bulb went on. I needed to be *seen* with an attractive guy. That way *I* would look attrac-tive. That was it! Just make sure I always had a good-looking boyfriend! (OK, so maybe I needed a little therapy, but it seemed like a logical solution at the time.)

I put this plan into action, and to my delight, I was able to find cute boys to hang around. During my junior year of high school, something changed though. There was a guy (oh, if I had a dime for every time a patient said this to me), Larry, who really liked me. I didn't have to play games to get him. Actually, I didn't even think about him—he was a sophomore, a grade behind me (how uncool would it be for me to even entertain liking him?). We were in the marching band together and he would talk to me on our way to the band room after practice. He pursued, and I could tell he was very interested in me. And he did meet my one criterion—he was nice-looking. So I nobly put our vast age difference (all of ten months) aside and eventually rewarded his persistence.

We became an item.

What I appreciated about Larry was that he made me feel special, even attractive. Funny thing, I didn't even think about my nose when I was with him. That could have been my first clue that body acceptance involves more than my own perceptions and self-observations, but did I notice? No! I concluded instead that being with an attractive man who thought I was attractive solved my problem. Little did I realize that the weakness in this thinking is that you always have to have that Larry person around to bolster your ego and reassure you that you make the cut.

You know what happened next, don't you? When Larry and I broke up during the last semester of my senior year, the insecurities returned. Maybe depending on a man to make you feel better about yourself was not a good idea. Fortunately, I didn't have to dwell on that thought too long! I was headed to college.

College provided a momentary break from my self-absorption because I simply had too many new things to concentrate on. But once I became more comfortable in my new world, the old nose insecurity returned with a vengeance. Distraction only works for a while.

The problem now was that all across campus, I kept running into those beautiful women with the perfect noses. Never mind that there were plenty of average-looking women like me. I only focused on the gorgeous ones. It was depressing. With so many sheer beauties around, it was time for yet another brilliant plan: to throw myself into becoming a scholar with lots of accomplishments. I figured that hard work and achievement might cure nose insecurities. If nothing else, they would certainly serve as my new distraction. As a therapist, I know now that detours are often the roads most traveled. And my nose dissatisfaction seemed to be leading me down one of those roads.

It had worked well for me in the past. When I felt bad about my physical body, I could look at my grades and feel better. You know the drill, don't you? Since I couldn't control the look of my nose, I would control something else.

Control—now there is a word we'll visit from time to time.

It's at the heart of most of our human problems. We think we have control even when we don't. And this belief often gets us in trouble. Control says, "Take charge of your life!" Yet it brings a certain despair that never quite goes away.

In college I was big on despair. I studied it in philosophy classes and became quite enamored with it as a necessary part of the human experience. "God is dead" had been the declaration on campuses only a decade earlier. Well, I knew He wasn't dead, but I wondered if He was paying attention.

My professors affirmed that He wasn't paying attention and that I was a fool to believe in such a delusion. Would a loving God who cared really allow all the suffering we saw in the world? Wasn't that proof enough that God isn't involved in our everyday lives?

For me, this question was more than an intellectual assent. It was personal. Only months before my freshman year of college, my oldest brother was killed in an airplane crash. I struggled with the fact that God did not stop my brother from dying an early death, despite his faith. I was confused and in despair, and my faith was shaken.

As I searched for answers as to why God had allowed one of His own to die young, I found many of the philosophers I was studying had answers, but they were depressing answers. The more I read about death, aloneness, and the emptiness of life, the more alienated I felt. So while I could relate to despair, I didn't enjoy feeling it. Deep inside I knew there was purpose even in tragedy and difficulty. There had to be. I just couldn't tell you what that was.

In response to all this confusion, I did what so many of us do when we grapple with life's questions—I protected myself from the pain by avoiding the real issue. The more I read of Nietzsche, Sartre, and other such philosophers, the more I was convinced that I had to take action on my own, construct my identity, be the master of my own fate, and all those other bumper sticker sayings that go along with commanding your destiny. Change, I reasoned, was a matter of will. If you don't like something, change it. Make it happen. Like my ancestors who came over from Germany, I could make choices that would create a better life. I just had to take control, because God didn't seem to be in charge. And in the midst of all that confusion, my nose dissatisfaction became a wonderful distraction. If I could fix how I looked, I reasoned, I would feel better.

That "pull yourself up by your bootstraps" approach sounded like needed relief, but could I *will* my nose to be different? No! How crazy was that? The practical side of this philosophy just wasn't working. And in reality, I wasn't taking control of anything either. All I was doing was whining about what I didn't like about my face and not dealing with the theological problem my brother's death posed to me.

By the grace of God, I never developed an eating disorder like so many of my friends. As I watched my girlfriends vomiting in the dorms and skipping meals in order to starve their bodies, I knew this kind of control was tempting but dangerous. Frankly, I'm afraid of danger. Even though I tried to make myself vomit a few times to see what the experience was like, I didn't like feeling sick. I felt more out of control than in control.

Either way, no amount of control would bring my brother back. Control was elusive anyway. Somewhere between pretending to take charge of my life and feeling hopeless about the future, there was an answer I needed to find.

Not only were my college professors influencing my beliefs, but pop culture weighed in as well. The message was that my identity could be constructed. In other words, I could be what I wanted to be. If I focused on my body and the way I looked, I would feel attractive, and thus I would be attractive. This thinking had a familiar ring from my high school days—be seen with an attractive guy and you will be attractive. I already knew this didn't work.

Obsessing about my looks wasn't helping me feel better about myself. In fact, it had the opposite effect. I finally realized I needed to confront the unfairness of life, whether it involved nose distribution or early death. For all my searching in books, help came in an unexpected place—a short book in the Bible that wasn't the subject of many sermons. Growing up in the church, I couldn't remember ever hearing a sermon from this book. All I knew about it was that the old 1960s song "There Is a Season" by the Byrds was based on a portion of it: "To everything, turn, turn, turn . . ." The helpful book was Ecclesiastes.

Let me warn you, Ecclesiastes isn't exactly devotional reading. When you want a lift in your mood, this is not the book to pick up and read with a peppermint mocha on a cold winter's night, especially if you have any propensity toward depression! This book is a bit sobering, but I liked that—I could relate to those feelings.

One of the mysterious things about Ecclesiastes is its authorship. Some scholars say King Solomon wrote it, others disagree. What's important is that the writer—a man called the Teacher— has experienced life to the fullest and shares his thoughts with us. After he informs us that "I never said no to myself. I gave in to every impulse, held back nothing" (2:10), he reports that this behavior resulted in feeling like his efforts were futile. He was bored with life. His conclusion is that everything is meaningless. Not exactly what you expect to hear from the Bill Gates of the Bible. It reminded me a lot of those existential guys I'd read in college.

The Teacher goes on to rant and rave about the injustices of life. The rich get richer; evil people don't get what they deserve; there is disease and world hunger; and the list goes on. Listen, noses or thighs are not specifically mentioned, but I figure that's because he was a guy! Had a woman written this book, body parts would have been involved!

What was the Teacher's advice? Eat, drink, and be happy, because tomorrow we are all going to die anyway. Had I stopped reading at that point, it would've been easy to think, *What's the point of college? What am I doing here trying to be an achiever? The Teacher studied, became wise, and found it was all a waste. Maybe I should learn by example. The "eat, drink, and be merry" parts are sounding better by the moment.*

Most of my fellow students were living by this philosophy anyway. And since I had no real control and injustice does prevail, what was the point of trying? More specifically, if my nose was beautiful or challenged, it really didn't matter.

You might think life is random and unfair, but in the middle of the book, the Teacher declares that life is filled with mysteries we cannot understand. The righteous may die young and the wicked may live a long life. Good people sometimes get bad noses. *But it's not because life is random.*

The Teacher had a different perspective than my college professors who droned on about the meaninglessness of life. The Teacher's instructions were to live in moderation and fear God. Don't give power to what others think and say, but be wise and submit to God and His way of doing things. Wisdom is better than foolishness, he said. Doing your best is good, but it's not the end-all.

And what is amazing about the Teacher's advice is that it came during a time of ultimate prosperity and progress for him and his country. His angst wasn't related to experiencing physical hardship or poverty like you might expect. He had reached the heights of what life had to offer in terms of wealth, achievement, wisdom, and every possible pleasure. Recall that he denied himself nothing. His question about the meaning of life came when he was at the top of his game, not the bottom.

I could relate. Not to being at the top, or the wealth and wisdom part, but to the fact that I, too, lived in a time of prosperity and social progress. And the intellectuals who were supposed to be preparing me for life outside the university were as confused as I was and pushing me to look for meaning in places that had already been visited. They didn't know what the Teacher knew—that anything apart from God leads to idolatry and emptiness, not answers. And certainly the culture around me wasn't clued in to this either. All it did was push the idea of beauty as the answer to any life problem. "Change the exterior and you'll feel better inside." Body idolatry definitely got the nod from popular culture.

In contrast, the Teacher says in the eighth chapter of Ecclesiastes that we can search as hard as we like to find the meaning of what God is doing on this earth, but we're not going to make sense of it. No matter how smart we are, we won't figure it out.

That's when I began to understand that philosophy and psychology didn't have the answers to all my questions. And the pursuit of the perfect nose or physical beauty wasn't going to cut it either. If physical beauty becomes my end goal, then I've lost sight of the One who created me. The pursuit of a perfect body part eventually results in a meaningless search.

Ecclesiastes 3:11 convinced me further, declaring, "He has made everything beautiful in its time" (NIV). It was time for me to accept my nose for what it was—not the result of a divine ADD moment, not something God intended to use to build my character—just a part of me. I needed to stop whining about it as a distraction from things I couldn't change. My full attention had to be toward God, not my body.

Really, my nose was leading me to the right place all along, to a focus on God and not me. This, I suspected, was a life lesson I would need to remember.

The final advice of the Teacher is, "Fear God. Do what he tells you" (12:13). The directive implies an acceptance of ourselves as mere creatures subject to God's great plan. In other words, we are to trust His grand plan even when we don't understand it, because God *is* paying attention. He may not always do things the way we would like, but we are mere creatures, not God. It's a powerful moment when you truly understand your place in the universe. *He is God and I am not.* That realization took a lot of pressure off me.

My nose also taught me that despair will not be cured by improved physical beauty or some other form of idolatry. Despair signals our need for God. When we try to go off on our own and find meaning by controlling our appearance, relationships, or some other substitute for God, we eventually come to the same conclusion as the Teacher. "All is vanity." Nothing will satisfy but God.

When we get this in our heads, we won't despair because we have the assurance that God uses the material of our lives, noses and all, to make something that has meaning and purpose. He has our lives in His control whether we believe it or not. Why not believe it and relax a little!

As Ecclesiastes proclaims, "There is a time to hold on and a time to let go" (3:6). Now is the time to let go and let God.

The rest of the story

When I married, my husband never commented on not liking my nose. It wasn't an issue. He thinks I'm beautiful, nose and all. Fortunately for him, it became less of an issue for me as I learned to accept those things I couldn't change. However, there is an ironic twist to my nose story.

Most of my life I had struggled with terrible sinus and allergy problems. To make matters worse, I live in one of the allergy capitals of America. I'd tried every preventative strategy I knew and complied with every regimen aimed at reducing the number of serious sinus infections I experienced. I took allergy shots for years, saw specialists, and even had CAT scans of my sinuses.

When all the scoping and scanning was done, my ear, nose, and throat doc (ENT) declared I had one of the worst deviated septums he'd ever seen! (See, I knew there was something up with my nose! I just didn't know it was on the inside rather than the outside. Remember that thought; it's a truth that applies in many areas of our lives.) The ENT was convinced that my inability to breathe through my nose was causing a number of these infections. Things just weren't draining properly.

This made sense. I always wondered why I ran with my mouth open. I noticed other runners didn't do this and would try to shut my mouth when I ran, but that only inhibited my ability to breathe. Now I knew why.

The ENT also decided that I couldn't continue to take so many antibiotics to treat my chronic infections, because I risked developing a growing tolerance to these important medications. The only way to help me with my ongoing sinus infections, he said, was to perform surgery on the interior of my nose. Desperate to get some relief, and tired of taking antibiotics almost monthly, I agreed.

When he reviewed the surgical procedure with me, he happened to mention that he would have to break my nose. "What!" I shouted. "How do you do that?"

This high-tech, best-in-his-field physician looked at me with a straight face and replied, "With a mallet. We break your nose with a mallet."

I started to laugh. "Right, modern medicine and a mallet. Come on, doc, how do you *really* do it?"

To my surprise, he wasn't kidding.

At that moment I realized I had made peace with my nose. I couldn't imagine anyone smashing it with a mallet. It seemed barbaric! Like most things, it's when you are about to lose them that you realize their true value.

"Can that not be avoided?" I inquired. "I mean, can you not correct the problem inside some other way? You don't know how long it's taken me to like this nose, and now you want to break it with a mallet? It's bad enough you need to do surgery, but hitting my nose with a mallet . . ."

"Linda, that's how it's done. The good news is that when we put it back together, it will probably look better than it does now. After smashing it, the plastics guy will make it look nice."

When I heard this, I sat there and started to laugh. All those years of struggle with my nose—coming to terms with my looks, accepting the way it was—was a moot point. Well, apparently not to God. *God, You have a really funny sense of humor.*

I'm happy to report that the surgery went well, although the pain afterwards was incredible. I looked like I had been punched out. In fact, whenever I ventured out during the healing, I'd receive one or two cards to a local shelter for battered women. I looked scary, and that in itself was a humbling thing.

A week after the surgery, when they pulled out all the gauze and material they had packed in my nose, the pain was worse than childbirth. But, like childbirth, the result was worth it. For the first time since I could remember, I could breathe through my nose like a normal person. The tiny bump was now gone too.

The process of acceptance had happened long before this moment. And I believe that was the point. I was led by my nose to true acceptance, and then God just had a little fun!

The Lesson

- God makes everything beautiful in its time.

CHAPTER 4

Breasts—What Would Barbie Do? (WWBD)

I think if you're beautiful in the United States . . .
you're built like Barbie.

—RENEE[1]

If the words "wardrobe malfunction" don't ring a bell, you must have been lost on a desert island to have missed all the fury that ensued when pop star Justin Timberlake peeled off a piece of Janet Jackson's clothing and exposed her breast during the halftime show of Super Bowl XXXVIII.

When Ms. Jackson violated the FCC regulations, an estimated 89 million viewers got a quick peek at her jewelry-studded breast. For those on the West Coast, this flicker of nudity took place during the dinner hour. Personally, I was deep in conversation with a neighbor and missed the moment. But my neighbor abruptly stopped the conversation and said, "Was that Janet Jackson's breast I just saw?"

It all goes to show that in spite of the nudity allowed elsewhere on television, baring your breasts can still get you noticed. Let's face it. Breasts create a lot of buzz whether they are the result of a wardrobe malfunction during the Super Bowl or because they are prominently displayed on the body of Barbie. Yes, Barbie. Even the Barbie doll—that classic symbol of Americana—joins the heat of controversy when it comes to breasts and body shape. With over a billion of them sold since their debut in 1959,[2] nipple-less Barbie is often cited as the bad girl of children's self-esteem. And the size of her breasts is part of the controversy.

You can't miss her, that's for sure! Barbie's real-life frame would stand about 5'9" with measurements of 36-18-33.[3] The worry over Barbie's breast size and other physical attributes relates to the influence Barbie may have on a child's developing self-concept, gender ideas, and body image. There is research that shows a connection between the doll's unrealistic measurements and body image.

For example, in a British study, over one hundred girls ages five to seven were given books to look at while being read a story about going shopping and to a birthday party. Some of the children received books with pictures of Barbie. Others had books without Barbie. (She must have been home in the Dream House.) According to the study, the girls who saw pictures of Barbie reported lower body esteem and had more of a desire to be thinner than those who looked at the books in which Barbie did not appear. From this, researchers concluded that early exposure to a doll with unrealistic body shape could damage the body image of girls.[4]

In her book *The Beauty Myth*, Naomi Wolf blames Barbie for the unrealisitic expectations girls develop in terms of their appearance. She proclaims the "official breast" is a "Barbie breast." Wolf argues that dolls like Barbie and other media influences heighten our anxieties about our bodies. Those who don't measure up to these unrealistic standards (which would be most of us) feel inadequate.

Part of the controversy is that Barbie is big, not only in breast size, but in popularity. She was included in America's 1976 bicentennial time capsule, and scores of the dolls now occupy about 4,000 square feet in the Toys "R" Us store in New York's Times Square.[5] That's a lot of real estate for a doll! Andy Warhol even painted a portrait of Barbie. And if you study a sociology course in any university, you are bound to examine Barbie as a gender image of popular culture.

Little girls love her. The average child between the ages of three and eleven owns ten Barbies.[6] Add the wardrobe (over one billion outfits in circulation) and accessories (1.2 million pairs of shoes and 35,000 handbags),[7] and you've got an impressive investment in a little girl's fantasy lifestyle. And why not? Barbie has it all—looks, fashion, cars, the boyfriend, and even multiple professional careers. Forget the glass ceiling. She's got expertise in over eighty career fields, my personal favorite being Paleontologist Barbie! Can't you just hear a four-year-old asking, "Mommy, what is a Pail and Toweling Barbie? Does she live at the beach?"

These pluses are the upside of Barbie mania, as some studies do show that playing with Barbie promotes dramatic play and language development among four-year–old children. Adult women who played with Barbie as a child report that their play was more about connection and opportunity versus looks.[8] After all, Barbie does have places to go, work to do, and people to see.

With all the controversy surrounding Barbie and body image, Mattel, the maker of Barbie, made some changes in 1998. The toy manufacturer came out with twenty-four new Barbie lines. Of those twenty-four, eight had modified body shapes—thicker waists, flatter feet (thank goodness the poor girl doesn't have to have her feet frozen in those 1.2 million high heels any longer!) and yes, smaller breasts. Now I know some of you are thinking, *Oh come on, she's only a harmless doll. An icon from the twentieth century. It's not like she's Chucky! Let her play in peace! Put on her yoga outfit and let's all calm down!*

The problem is that Barbie's unrealistic body proportions do impact the thinking of young girls. And her buxom breasts are like two torpedoes capable of launching a pop culture debate. Some would even argue that Barbie could be influencing women toward breast implants—that seeing those giant breasts as a child may make us desire them as adults.

I was given a Barbie doll growing up. Notice I said "a" Barbie. Mine was the original version. She had black hair, a black and white-striped swimsuit, earrings that looked like the tops of straight pins, open-toed shoes, and sunglasses. Just a side note: There were no redheaded Barbies back in my day! Go figure!

Now, don't get excited if you are a collector reading this. Here's why. One day during my childhood, I decided to see what Barbie's hairstyle looked like when it wasn't pulled up in that signature ponytail. It was my own shock and awe moment. Barbie was bald at the top of her head, and no matter how hard I tried, I could not get her hair back to its original ponytail! Bald spaces spread between the hair strands like opened shutters. Perhaps this is why I am not so strictly against Barbie; I feel for her and her flawed hair. Hey, at least I noticed she was flawed!

Like most of the girls in my neighborhood, I played with Barbie, but I wasn't enamored with her. I preferred real people who didn't wear high heels and could play a game of tag. But I did have my Barbie moments, and I have to admit I was fascinated by her breast size. Then again, the women in my family were quite well-endowed, and so Barbie's breasts weren't a stretch for my imagination.

Even though I ruined Barbie by unstyling her hair, I have a hard time believing she ruined *me*. I know there are feminists who believe Barbie is the root of all body image evil. I will concede that staring at her naked body probably influenced my thinking about the feminine ideal—although for me, it was her thighs more than her breasts! That said, I am not convinced that all my body image angst was caused by a doll. Frankly, Barbie's name has never come up in the twenty-five years I've conducted therapy with women. I just don't believe she has that much power. But when you add Barbie to all the other cultural prescriptions for breast size, perhaps you've got a force with which to reckon.

Without being an alarmist, it is important to recognize that children's toys do influence the development of self-concept.[9] But hold on—you don't have to burn one of Barbie's bead-studded bras in protest! That fact doesn't mean girls are going to request breast implants because of a doll. It's more likely that the combined images of dolls, magazines, movies, and other media add up to the message that big breasts are desirable.

So the primary question is, "What would Barbie do" if she could walk and talk and give us her perspective? Of course, we would have to consult Psychologist Barbie to know the answer, but here are my guesses.

First, she would administer a battery of psychological tests to all girls who played with her in order to ensure they aren't being harmed by her image. After interpreting all the ink blots, she would schedule breast reduction surgery for herself in order to avoid incredible back pain as she ages. Next, she would warn young girls about being too thin, stating that the thinness of her waist and hips makes menstruation difficult. (We all need some fat on our frames to keep the plumbing working well.) Barbie would then set up a nonprofit arm of Mattel that would donate proceeds of her sales to eating disorder research, and she would most likely convert the Dream House to a group home for troubled girls. Regular group therapy would be held there in order to help girls deal with unrealistic body image. Community seminars would explain her evolution into a doll with more sensible proportions.

My guess is she would also request that Mattel make a size 12 Barbie with size A breasts—a doll that more closely resembles mom.

Now I know I am going to receive mail on this, so I might as well address it now. For those of you wondering if I allowed my daughter to have a Barbie doll, wonder no more. If you have children and you've ever thrown them a birthday party, it is impossible not to have Barbie show up among the gifts. The reason the average child has ten Barbies is probably because she gets so many from her friends at birthday parties! From the ages of three to eleven, birthdays are a Barbie binge!

Gymnast Barbie was my daughter's favorite. She only cared about how well Barbie could turn flips and do the splits. I can't remember her commenting on Barbie's body except to point out her humongous breasts. However, we did talk about Barbie's pretend body and the fact that real women don't look like her. It was an easy sell because she had only to look at her mother to know that was the truth!

After several discussions about Barbie's body, my daughter finally said, "I get it. We don't look like Barbie, and that's fine! Mom, I really don't want to look like Barbie anyway, but I sure do want to tumble like she does!" And that's the point summed up by a six-year-old—most real people don't look like her and never will. Barbie is a fantasy doll. But the additional message needs to be, "To look like Barbie means you'd have to starve, compulsively exercise, and agree to breast implants! But to what end?

To meet some idealistic cultural standard decided by whom? Men, the media, the porn industry?"

Unfortunately, some women will try to look like Barbie no matter how unhealthy her body frame is. And getting breast implants is part of the look. However, Barbie isn't the only large-breast inspiration for young girls today.

Pop stars like Britney Spears, Lindsay Lohan, and others who boost their busts become role models along with celebrities like Pamela Anderson. Advertisements for the Wonder Bra tell us to make our breasts look bigger. The Victoria's Secret models strut their padded bras to the hilt. Television casts beautiful women wearing plunging necklines and too-tight sweaters as reporters and sitcom regulars. These constant images play into a reality that big is better when it comes to breasts. And that reality can come crashing home in our teenagers. Let's check out a few of their stories.

> *"I have no chest. I am planning to have surgery. I'm going to fix this."*
>
> —MEGAN[10]

Sweet sixteen is a birthday most of us remember. When you turned sixteen, what gift did you ask for? New clothes, a car, a computer, a special party, a music system? A few years ago, one British teen shocked the world when she made her special birthday request. Fifteen-year-old Jenna Franklin asked for breast enlargements for her sixteenth birthday. Specifically, Jenna wanted to go from a size 34A to a 34C or D. Forget the new T-shirt, she wanted new breasts to fit into it! Incidentally, her boyfriend was supportive of the idea (now there's a real shocker!).

Apparently Jenna had been thinking about the operation

since she was twelve years old. What's even more remarkable is that her then forty-year-old mother supported her request, and her father agreed to pay for the surgery. Dad believed his daughter was old enough (at the ripe old age of fifteen) to make such a decision and that getting implants would increase her confidence. It seems Mrs. Franklin had gone under the knife for two breast implant operations herself. Mom wanted her daughter to avoid any hang-ups she might have about her looks, stating, "I want her to feel confident about the way she looks, and if that means having breast implants, then so be it."[11] Note to the Franklin family: Please call me for family therapy!

Fortunately, both parents had a moment of sanity when they agreed to listen to the advice of plastic surgeons before granting Jenna's request. The Franklins hand-picked Dr. Anthony Erian. He felt Jenna was too young for breast implants and noted that her breasts were still developing. He also mentioned that she could experience mental and physical implications from the surgery. Consequently, he declined to perform the operation and the parents agreed to wait a few years. Because the story made headlines, the British Association of Plastic Surgeons responded, affirming that breast augmentation should not be carried out at so young an age.

Even though the surgery was delayed, I want you to hear the thoughts of this fifteen-year–old because they worry me. Jenna defended her decision by saying, "You've got to have big breasts to be successful. I used to pray my boobs would grow. Then I just thought, what's the point when I can have implants when I want? I just want to be happy with my body and I think having my breasts enlarged will give me more self-confidence."[12]

Close that dropped jaw and understand that this mixed-up child is not an unattractive, overweight teen. She looked like a "normal" fifteen year old when I saw her picture. I was stunned that she even had the thought of changing her breasts. They looked fine to me. (I wonder if she played with ten Barbies as a child.)

And then there was the case of a Quebec teen who had breast implant surgery at the expense of the provincial health board known in Canada as the *Régie de l'assurance maladie du Québec*. The board approved this teen's surgery after her parents brought a note from a psychiatrist saying the child's small breasts were harming her mental and emotional stability. *Harming her mental and emotional stability?* Now it's time for me to close my dropped jaw.

When this request was made, the head of the Quebec Association of Plastic Surgeons responded by saying that self-image problems related to breast size could be improved by surgery.[13]

It's frightening, isn't it? The thinking of these teens, professionals, and parents is sad. But I wonder how much these two teens reflect the world they see? One has to question if it is really their insecurity talking or perhaps their reality speaking. Most likely, it's a combination of both.

Given our current cultural climate, it isn't too far a stretch to see how a sixteen-year-old could believe popularity wears big breasts. Even in a teen's world of school and friends, big breasts are huge attention-grabbers. And sadly, girls don't seem to grasp that self-confidence is the last thing on the mind of boys who gawk at them.

I understand how teens can be confused, but what I don't get is the lack of common sense by parents. Why would any parent consult a surgeon to solve his or her daughter's lack of self-confidence . . . and believe bigger breasts are the answer? It's absurd, and the message couldn't be more disturbing. If you believe big breasts bring self-confidence, I've got a Tooth Fairy for rent!

How have we gotten to the point that a teen's body, still not yet fully developed, is treated like a mistake in need of correction?

Women's breasts don't fully develop until around age twenty-one, and some not until their mid-twenties, and yet the number of teen breast implants has tripled in the past few years.[14] The reasons most teens give for wanting breast implants is to boost their self-confidence and self-esteem.

If breast implants are sought in order to improve self-esteem, they won't fix the problem. In fact, this procedure is a dangerous way to deal with a teen's or adult's anxiety, and it often results in a decline in mental health, not an improvement. There is even research indicating that patients who had breast augmentation are four times more likely to commit suicide when compared to other plastic surgery patients.[15]

Implants don't last a lifetime either. In all likelihood, one will break within 7-12 years and need to be replaced in a second operation. This means that on top of the original surgery cost of between $4,000-$6,000, you have to factor in repair and replacement costs and health risks.[16] Are we talking about cars or people here? Furthermore, implants can become hard and make breast cancer detection more difficult. And there is a possibility that you may not be able to breastfeed.

The questions to ask are:

- Is it worth it?
- Why are we doing this?

I watched an interview on MTV with a young pop star who claimed her breast implants were a feminist act—that the only reason she had the surgery was to feel empowered. She was doing this incredible thing for herself. *For herself?* Really.

I wanted to shake her and her large breasts and say, "Come on! If you lived on an island with all women, would you be having a boob job for yourself? If you weren't in the business of selling millions of CDs through music videos, would you be doing this for yourself? What is empowering about selling out to a cultural ideal? Especially before your breasts are even fully developed! If you want to be empowered, look at your natural breasts in the mirror and say, 'These are great.'"

Getting to normal

Not too long after Jenna Franklin's birthday wish made the news, a British documentary called *Perfect Breasts* aired that addressed this growing trend of young girls opting for breast enhancement. A number of girls and women were interviewed who hated their bodies and just wanted to look, well, normal.

In the documentary there is a disturbing dinner scene between two sisters and their parents. Both sisters have breast implants. As the family is discussing various topics, the parents raise the possibility that the girls may never be able to breastfeed a baby due to the implants. The younger sister isn't bothered by this at all. In fact, she thinks using her breasts for nourishment is repulsive. Giggling, she comments that her breasts are sex objects. Her nervous father just mumbles and tries to raise a mild protest.[17]

Caroline Prest, who was also interviewed for the documentary, had a different story. She pestered her parents for breast implants for two years until they finally relented. At the age of seventeen, she had the operation. Was she happy with her decision? Only a month passed before the novelty of what she had done wore off. What resulted wasn't peace. Instead, she developed a fixation on a different part of her body. A few years later she realized how off her perceptions were about her body. Looking at old pictures before the implant surgery, she couldn't believe she once thought she needed to make changes. Her breasts looked fine. Now, realizing that men look at her breasts and not her face is an unsettling fact.[18]

It's true that girls have been stuffing their bras since the 1950s and 1960s in an effort to look buxom. The difference is that the stuffing could always be pitched in the trash once you realized how ridiculously you were behaving. Not so with surgery. So I'm asking us to think about *why* we desire breast implants.

Why do most of the women on the extreme makeover shows get implants when their breasts look perfectly fine? Why are we willing to succumb to someone else's ideal of the perfect woman?

The decision to change your breasts is highly personal. I get that. I'm not here to heap condemnation or guilt on those of you who have augmented your breasts. I just want us to think about the reasons behind elective breast surgery, especially for those who appear "normal" but desire to "improve" their appearance.

When I think we are all headed for the surgeon's office, I'm encouraged by young teens like Denise Fuller. She has an attitude we all need to adopt. She talks about being thirteen, but her comments could apply to any age. "When you're thirteen and just getting used to the changing world around you, the last thing you need is the constant reminder of what you are not, and what you and hundreds of others wish they could be but most likely will never become."[19] Congratulations to Denise's parents. They are raising a clear-thinking daughter in the midst of cultural craziness.

As women, we have to ask why small breasts are not acceptable. Who says they aren't, and why will we risk our physical and mental health to comply with some crazy notion that our designed bodies need to be fixed?

Our breasts are not sexual objects or toys. Now I don't mean that our breasts aren't feminine or can't be sexual in the right expression of a committed relationship. But we need to keep in mind that our breasts were also designed with a purpose—to breastfeed and nurture babies. This isn't disgusting like the uninformed teen with breast implants proclaimed. It's beautiful. And even if you choose not to have children, small breasts have certain advantages. You don't have to wear a bra if you don't want to. You avoid back pain and posture problems associated with large breasts. You can jog and not hurt!

You might have noticed I have been quite silent about my own personal struggles with accepting my breasts. This is because this isn't a body part I dislike. I've always liked my breasts. And when the time came to nurse both of my children, I couldn't wait for the opportunity. It was one of the most rewarding experiences I've ever had and far from the negative sentiment voiced by the young teen with implants.

Now it's true that the after-effects of nursing left me a bit disappointed and challenged my body image a bit. My breast size shrunk, and of course there was the sagging. But the experience of bonding with and nurturing new lives was well worth the aftermath. And I adjusted and had a new appreciation for my breasts. My changing body was part of the natural progression and circle of life.

We all get to experience the pull of gravity on our breasts. Over time those perky twosomes begin to sag as the skin loses its elasticity. With aging and multiple breastfed babies, I know this is when many women consider a breast lift. But before you feel the need to lift and move your nipples (that thought just makes me squeamish!), consider the sagging as a normal part of aging and an opportunity to embrace a new season in your own life.

Self-Examination

I worked on this chapter during October, Breast Cancer Awareness Month. While I've always supported breast cancer research, this year held special significance. My sister-in-law, Bevie Jo, was diagnosed with breast cancer. Now facing surgery, chemotherapy, and radiation, her life changed the moment she felt that lump under her arm.

If you knew my sister-in-law, you would never guess her age. She's fifty-two years old and looks about thirty-two. Cute as a button, always fit and trim and careful about her body, she is now facing the challenge that every woman with breast cancer faces. Her appearance will be altered due to the chemotherapy, surgery, and radiation. The body takes a toll when cancer is involved— scarring, changes to the skin after radiation, hair loss from chemotherapy, weight changes. And the toll isn't just physical; it's spiritual and emotional as well.

As I thought about the coming days for my sister-in-law, I thought about the number of women that I know who, for the first time, had to look at their altered breasts in the mirror or reveal them to an intimate partner after surgery. I thought not only about the loss of a breast, but of the hair and weight loss that accompany chemotherapy. And I remembered the number of husbands who had told me in therapy that the changes in their wives' breasts didn't stop them from loving their wives or appreciating them even more. Life was more important than the loss of a breast or the disfigurement it caused.

Many of those husbands felt desperate to help their wives believe that they were less bothered by the physical changes than their wives were. They wanted their wives to know that when they said, "You are still beautiful to me," they meant it. And they longed for their wives to see what they saw—a new beauty emerging from the courage and strength of these women as they fought the cancer in their bodies.

To be faced with the surgical removal of a lump, a breast, or both breasts is daunting for any woman. We like our breasts, and when we lose them, the change in appearance takes a lot of getting used to. As difficult as that adjustment is for most women, it strengthens some to no longer care what others say about their femininity. Courageously, they learn to accept their bodies unconditionally and let go of former insecurities.

The reality of breast cancer forces women to face a truth that all women must face: that we are accepted unconditionally, no matter what our breast size may be. God's acceptance is far greater than any we garner from other people. It is where we find our anchor. It penetrates our spirits, frees us emotionally, and renews our minds. It reminds us that body image is more about what's in the mind and spirit than what we see in the mirror. God esteems us for who we are, no matter what happens to our outward appearance. Like the emotionally healthy men who tell their breast cancer-surviving wives, "You are beautiful to me," God stands by all women and proclaims the same.

What would Barbie do?

Strangely, my ponderings about breast size brought me back full circle to Barbie. Ruth Handler, Barbie's inventor, developed breast cancer later in life and underwent a modified radical mastectomy. The evolution of her own thinking is evident in the remarks she made: "When I conceived Barbie, I believed it was important to a little girl's self-esteem to play with a doll that has breasts. Now I find it even more important to return that self-esteem to women who have lost theirs."[20]

Handler redirected her efforts from developing dolls with big breasts to developing a line of breast prostheses she called Nearly Me. The company, although resold several times, exists today.

So what would Barbie do? The question has been answered. Barbie met breast cancer and refocused her life. As a result, her decision is clear: She would encourage all of us to accept our breasts for what they are. To look to our Maker for unconditional love and support. And to resist cultural prescriptions that say big is better.

The Lessons

- Big is not better, it's just bigger.
- Refocus your life on more important issues. You are already accepted and cherished.

CHAPTER 5

Stomach Aches

Growing up, I was a healthy kid but every once in awhile ate too many sour cherries or inhaled a mess of candy at the county fair. Those days usually ended with me in bed, moaning and groaning from an upset stomach.

Well, we aren't kids anymore, but some of us are still moaning and groaning because of our stomachs. Growing up hasn't cured us. We've just got a new kind of stomach ache—one that comes from not liking what we see in the mirror between our waists and our pelvises. In fact, the most disliked body part of them all is (drumroll, please,) . . . you guessed it, the stomach.[1] I really thought it would be those thighs! Our stomachs can be a pain when it comes to liking what we see in the mirror. But the relief we need doesn't come from a bottle!

In America, we believe in the myth that the only good stomach is a flat stomach! The "six pack" or "washboard" abs are envied and highly celebrated. Usually these are developed by people who live in the gym and compete in body-building contests or who model fitness products. But for most of us, flat stomachs don't come naturally. Still, we covet flat abs along with the "perfect female" body measurements of 36-24-36, which, incidentally, requires a size 2 waist above that flat stomach. Is it any wonder that our stomachs ache!

Treating stomach aches

A woman's stomach is unique. From menarche to menopause, it's the one area of a woman's body guaranteed to change whether we like it or not. *And this is normal.*

During puberty, a young girl's body changes to prepare for pregnancy. These changes include a widening of the hips, a narrowing of the waist, and fat being stored in the stomach. As the reproductive organs mature, the onset of menstruation brings about cramping and bloating of the stomach for a day or two. The excess fluid leaves us feeling fat and unattractive until the bloating finally goes away.

Because of the pain and cramping we learn to associate with our stomachs at this time, we have to be careful not to begin to dislike our stomachs and view them as the monthly enemy. They are actually doing us a favor by automatically preparing our bodies for possible pregnancy.

When pregnant, a woman's growing stomach represents fertility and new life. This reality should be celebrated and not held in disdain. Thanks to the hormone relaxin, our stomach muscles know pregnancy means it's time for the stomach to relax! As the belly expands with the growing baby, we wonder if we'll ever see our waists again. Again, this is normal, but the change in our waistlines takes some adjusting. And to our further dismay, the stomach muscles lose some of their elasticity postpartum. And with every baby, a bit of a bulge will remain as a small badge of honor.

I'm saddened when I hear young adult women talk about pregnancy as an inconvenience or hindrance to body acceptance. Rather than celebrate our maturing journey through adulthood, pregnancy is seen as something to overcome as quickly as possible. As soon as the baby is delivered, there is this cultural expectation that we should all look like Demi Moore did after she delivered her baby. But how many of us have her luxuries of a personal trainer and being able to exercise three hours a day, or would choose to spend that much time working out with a new baby around anyway? Maybe the expectation is unrealistic.

Even those of us who manage to maintain relatively flat abs for most of our young adult life eventually succumb to the stomach changes of midlife. The third stomach transition comes during the aging process associated with pre-menopause and menopause. If you are between the ages of thirty-five and fifty-five, welcome to the age of the inevitable expanding waistline.

When metabolisms slow down in this season of a woman's life, less estrogen is produced and weight can get stored in the stomach, especially if that is your genetic propensity, you have poor nutrition, and/or you exercise very little. The key is to keep up exercise (especially strength training) and eat better, but also to recognize that the shifting of weight to the stomach is normal.

According to Mary Ann Mayo and her husband Dr. Joseph Mayo in their helpful book *The Menopause Manager*, the average woman gains about ten pounds during this phase of life and a possible five more if surgical menopause is in the picture. And this added weight tends to accumulate at the waist and stomach.[2] Maybe this is why we don't see middle-aged women modeling bathing suits!

Now I have to admit, this is not great news, but it does explain why trimming the waist is harder to do later in life. But wait, there's more! Your waist size and waist-to-hip ratio are predictors of coronary heart disease.[3] So if you have that classic apple- versus pear-shaped body, you are more at risk for health problems. And to top it off, stress can increase your abdominal fat. When cortisol is released during stressful times, it tends to stimulate the storage of fat around your belly. This may be the body's way of shutting down the stress response.[4] So there you have it—stress can make you fat!

OK, now that we are full of great news and good cheer, what do we do about all this? First, we have to understand the natural course of growth and development in the female body and learn to accept it. Maybe that doesn't seem fair. Personally, I hated reading that statistic about the expanding waistline in midlife. But I had to ask myself why it bothered me so much. I mean, who decided that the right stomach is a flat stomach, especially when this isn't the natural state for most women?

The rock-hard stomach sounds good in theory. The problem is that acquiring this look just isn't going to happen for most of us. The abdominal muscles form a rounded shape, not a flat one. And the size and shape of your abdominal muscles are impacted by your age and body type.

Even taking up residence at a local gym won't achieve the washboard abs we see on swimsuit models. Flat abs are apparently genetically bestowed. Biology is destiny!

As women, we are simply designed to store fat in our stomachs. Think about it. Physiology and genetics, pregnancies, weak abdominal muscles, being overweight, or losing a massive amount of weight and the resulting loose skin all work against the flat stomach. For many of us, the flat stomach will not be physiologically possible to attain, much less maintain, and we are wasting time going after it. That said, there are still measures we can and should take.

Back to stomachs

Over a year and a half ago, I began to feel pain in my hip area when I sat at my desk. At the time I was writing a book and spent hours each day in front of my computer. At first I didn't think anything about the pain and figured I just needed to get up from my chair and move around more often.

As the days passed, though, the pain worsened. Eventually, I began rolling on the floor every thirty minutes or so to ease the discomfort on my right side. After about a week, I was having difficulty sitting in my chair for any length of time and found that standing up and lying down were the only comfortable positions. The pain continued to worsen and became more intense until one day I couldn't get out of bed.

My best guess was that I pulled a muscle, or maybe something in my hip was out of alignment, so I called my chiropractor. After several treatments with no real pain relief, he referred me for an MRI, believing something more than chiropractic was needed. By now I was dealing with nonstop pain that was becoming unbearable. My right foot had gone numb, the excruciating pain in my leg was unrelenting, and my back throbbed day and night. With no history of back or hip problems and no recollection of a recent injury, I couldn't imagine what was causing me the problem, although eventually I remembered that several months earlier, I had fallen hard while ice-skating and trying to do a flying camel.

The MRI revealed a massive bulge sitting on my sciatic nerve and oozing out from the L5 vertebrae of my lower back. There was only one recommendation made by all the doctors I consulted: immediate surgery.

Neurosurgery! That sounded a little too drastic to me. How about some injections, physical therapy, rest? But I was told that delays in removing the bulge could leave me incontinent and damage the nerves in my right leg. The longer I waited, the more likely that the damage would be permanent or irreversible.

Despite my objections, I could see no other option unless God healed me immediately. That was my constant prayer. "God, just take Your finger and move that bulge back into my vertebrae and everything will be fine." I knew God could do this. It was a small act for a big God, so for thirty days I waited on Him.

Since I couldn't tolerate any of the pain medications I tried, what carried me through those thirty days of physical torture was distraction, constant prayer, and the compassion of a physician who practiced acupuncture. May God bless Dr. Su for explaining acupuncture to me in scientific terms (he is a physician) and relieving the pain in my leg temporarily.

In all that time, my faith never questioned what God could do. The night before the scheduled surgery, I really thought God had healed me. I walked around the house for the first time in thirty days with very little pain, thinking that if I woke up like this the next morning, I'd cancel the operation. Come the next day, the pain was back with a vengeance. God, in His mercy and grace, had given me a brief respite and a good night's sleep but apparently planned for me to be healed through surgery. So I had surgery.

It went well, as did my recovery. But the change in my physical activity (which went from very active to basically zero) changed my body. I had to limit my movement for months. As a result, my arms became flabby and, for the first time in my life, I developed a protruding stomach. And this bothered me.

Now you would think that getting pain relief, correcting a serious problem, and coming through the surgery would completely eliminate any thoughts of body image. I should have just been happy to walk again relatively pain-free! But here's where the cultural programming rears its ugly head from time to time:

I didn't want a protruding stomach; I just wanted my old stomach back. Hadn't I been through enough?

Sounds pretty shallow, doesn't it? I had just come through this incredible experience, and I could feel God's presence like no other time in my life. And *now* I was being distracted by a slight bulge in my midsection! And to make matters worse, it coincided with the physical changes I was experiencing related to being in my late forties. The girth of my middle was spreading ever so much on a part of my body I used to like.

What I learned was that we are never too old to begin obsessing on any body part! We need to be aware of this and keep up our guard.

Recently on *Living the Life*,[5] we did a show on midlife stress. To prepare for the show, I read up on the body changes associated with this stage of life and discovered that our abdominal walls become weaker as we age. This is what causes a protruding stomach. Exercise is one way to strengthen those muscles and maintain their tone.

Prior to back surgery I had no trouble lifting weights and doing crunches. After surgery I was afraid I would injure myself. But now more than ever, I needed to strengthen my abdominal muscles in order to help my back. Plus, I wanted to fix my flabby stomach.

During that adjustment period after surgery I was once again faced with a familiar choice. Would I do the right thing for my body because my body needed it, or would I get back in shape just so I could look good again? This time, exercise was not about looking good or sculpting my body to some mediated image; it was about restoring my strength and health.

Please, exercise to be toned and healthy, not because you are driven by some crazy notion that your stomach is bad and needs to be flatter. In my case, exercise not only helped my bad back

WARNING!

Let me say this about exercise. It is a good thing when it's done for the right reasons. It can become a compulsion when it's motivated by a fear of getting fat or refusal to accept our imperfections. I am reminded of all the anorexics I have treated who compulsively exercise. At medically dangerous low weights, they see any natural showing of the stomach as fat and often engage in intense exercise as a way to burn calories. It's typical for an anorexic woman to do compulsive sit-ups every night, run marathons, or be unable to sleep until she has spent significant time in the gym.

The obsession with exercise is a distraction for them. The anorexic woman's motivation for compulsive exercise has to do with keeping the body childlike and represents her need to repress her sexuality, control her life, attempt to cope with stress, and create an identity (albeit a false one) through thinness and dependence. It has nothing to do with being healthy. ❧

but also toned my muscles, got my heart pumping, increased my circulation, and improved my mood. Yet it didn't melt away my tummy entirely. And that's another reality I had to accept.

Even when we exercise, we have to surrender to the process of aging. I at first feared that my stomach muscles had turned to fat when I was flat on my back for months, but once I discovered the facts, I realized they don't change magically to fat. No, the change was in part due to aging. What didn't go away and tone up post-op was nothing more than that. My age was showing.

Still, having gone through that ordeal, I am a firm believer that the size of our stomachs should not determine our self-confidence or happiness. And hopefully by the end of this chapter you'll be in that camp too.

Toning, not moaning and groaning

If we try to lose weight as a way to flatten our stomachs, it may not work, because we don't always lose weight where we want to lose it and because exercise doesn't necessarily reduce abdominal fat. Furthermore, special diets and expensive equipment aren't going to automatically make you fall in love with your stomach. But exercise will tone your abdominal muscles. And it is good for your lower back and posture.

The American Council on Fitness tells us that sit-ups and crunches do help tighten our abs.[6] But "tighter abs" refers to tightening the *muscles*, not the *fat*. You don't tighten fat, regardless of what infomercials might lead you to believe! If you don't like your stomach, exercise your abdominal muscles for the health benefit this provides.

Make sure you use the proper technique. Here's a sample of what the experts recommend. Go ahead, get on the floor, and try these if your health permits:

"Lie on your back with knees bent, feet flat on the floor, hands across the chest, and elbows out straight. Raise your shoulders off the floor toward your knees by curling your upper back off the floor. (Note: It is not necessary to completely raise the chest and upper trunk to a sitting position during an abdominal curl, as it causes no further contraction of abdominal muscles.) Aim for 10 repetitions a day and gradually increase to 20 to 30 repetitions a day, which is usually sufficient for strengthening abdominal muscles.

"If you place your hands behind your head instead of across the chest during a curl, be careful not to pull the neck and create stress on the cervical vertebrae. Many abdominal exercisers are designed to prevent neck stress and help you stay in the right position. Also, avoid fast, twisting motions and never continue an exercise that hurts or causes pain. Remember that straight-leg sit-ups are a no-no, fitness experts emphasize, because they put extreme pressure on your lower back."[7]

After you've finished a round of crunches, get up off the floor and check your thinking. Are you doing this to tone up and improve your overall health, or were you motivated by hating your imperfect stomach? If you are still struggling, I want you to look at your babies, big or small. Was a little stomach pooch worth those precious lives? If you don't have babies, look at the women you most admire in life. Do you zero in on their stomachs as a way to determine if you should admire them? Of course not!

The point is that we've been hooked by the myth of the flat stomach. We've swallowed the bait, and now it's time to reclaim our stomachs as our own. Flat, protruding, or somewhere in-between, don't treat your stomach like a foreign object. Pat it, rub it, and try to like it! Its expansions have grand significance for the female form.

Oh, and one final suggestion: do like a fish. I'm serious! Read on.

Something fishy

When I was researching this chapter, I found an unlikely source of help in an article about fishing, a topic that usually puts me to sleep. The article was about what to do with a fish once you've caught it and want to return it to its natural habitat or state. This topic grabbed my interest because that's my M.O. on the rare occasions when I do fish—I want to return the flapper to the water so it can find Nemo and the rest of its buddies and quit staring at me with its bulging eyes.

When you reel in a fish from the deep, not only are its eyes bulging, but its stomach is sticking out of its mouth! I know this sounds really gross, but since we are talking about stomachs, and it reminded me of us women, I kept reading. Who knew fish stomachs bloated too?

The reason the fish's stomach does this is because of something that happens to the swim bladder, an organ found in the abdominal cavity. Apparently when fish aren't being bothered by humans, this swim bladder is relatively small due to the pressure of the water compressing the gases in the abdominal cavity. But when the fish is quickly brought to the water's surface, then those gases expand and can even burst. This causes the poor fishy's abdomen to bloat and swell, and as you can guess, this is not good for his survival.

Ah, but there is help for that fish who thinks it's about to meet its Maker—if the fisherman will vent those gases and release the pressure on the stomach. And you have to do it the *right* way or the fish becomes your next round of bait! Now stick with me; it'll all make sense in a moment.

Here are the two things that you are *not* supposed to do when face to face with a caught fish:

1. Try and force its stomach back into its body.
2. Puncture its stomach to release the gases.

In either case, the fish might swim away but die later.[8]

Taking the bait

By now, this is probably more fish information than you ever wanted to know, but this fish story does relate to us in terms of how we feel about and deal with our own stomachs. Like fish that have been reeled to the surface, we have been caught by the superficiality of the culture. The bait (the notion that the only right stomach is a flat one) has been placed on the hook, and we've swallowed it whole.

When our stomachs don't measure up to this cultural stereotype, we flop around like fish out of water, struggling for emotional survival. We'll do whatever it takes, healthy or unhealthy, to get that stomach moved back into its determined place.

Intuitively, we know that disliking our stomachs is not healthy and that we need better ways to live with the stomachs we've been given. Just as a fish needs to be vented properly, we must properly vent the cultural "think" out of our minds in order to survive. In other words, we need to stop taking the bait and be more realistic about this important body part called the stomach.

Like our fish friends, our emotional survival is dependent on making changes the right way. We can look to the fish story for a few pointers. Consider the two "do nots" mentioned above. First, we are told not to try stuffing the stomach back into the body. Open any catalogue for women's lingerie and you'll see numerous contraptions and garments aimed at doing just this. From the corset to the girdle, women have been stuffing their rounded stomachs into their bodies for ages. Next time you consider buying one of these crazy undergarments, remember today's illustration and tell yourself, "Hmm, it sounds fishy to me!"

I've got this one girdle that will slim out my stomach and thighs and make a smooth line for my dresses. I wore it once to an event that lasted a number of hours, and boy, was I sorry! By the time I came home, I had marks on my body that looked like I had been tattooed. And my stomach hurt so bad that I thought we needed to stop at the emergency room and have this thing cut off me. Only the Jaws of Life could help me breathe!

Second, we are instructed to avoid puncturing the fish's stomach. The application for us humans is obvious: avoid the scalpel if you can. I'm not saying that you should never consider a tummy tuck, but you should consider the risks and the reasons you want to do it. Your stomach gets cut, and fat and skin are removed from the abdominal wall. This is not like getting a pedicure, and it isn't a weight reduction strategy either. In my mind, it's like puncturing the fish. It has risks—bleeding, infection, and blood clots—and sometimes people die.[9]

I know of a woman who died from a blood clot weeks after the surgery. Now I realize she was the exception to the rule, and

I don't tell you this to scare you, but elective plastic surgery has risks and we all need to think about these risks before we allow someone to take a scalpel to our bellies. Let's be informed about the choices we make.

Certainly we don't want surgery for the wrong reasons. So what are the wrong reasons? Well, a conversation between two friends like the one below fits the category. Listen in.

DENISE: "Do I look fat today? I really feel fat. My stomach is huge; I hate it. Don't you just hate your stomach?"

CLARA: "Denise, your stomach looks fine."

DENISE: "I just can't get it to go flat. There is this twenty-three-year-old chick at work who goes to the gym every night and works out like a maniac. Her stomach is as hard as a rock. I can't go to the gym every night, and yet this is what I'm competing with. But I can't compete with this body. I just can't."

CLARA: "I'm sorry, what are you competing with—the twenty-three-year-old? You mean for a guy?"

DENISE: "Of course I mean for a guy! I can't get a decent man to look at me at work when I've got these twenty-something-year-olds running around flaunting their workout bodies. I was thinking about a tummy tuck. I'm thirty-four, and it may be time to start making some improvements. That would probably solve the problem and boost my confidence."

CLARA: "What? A tummy tuck? You know it's not like getting a new haircut. It's major surgery with risks and scars. You haven't even had children yet. And do you really think a tummy tuck will get men to pay more attention to you and bring in Mr. Right?"

DENISE: "Maybe."

CLARA: "Are you kidding?"

DENISE: "OK. No. I hate it when you are so sensible. Sounds pretty lame, doesn't it? But I've always hated my stomach. What about liposuction then?"

CLARA: "Denise, stop! Your stomach is fine. It's not supposed to be rock-hard like those women in the gym. They exercise four to five hours a day. Who can do that? Who *wants* to do that? And even if you did, you might not end up looking like them anyway. You probably have to be born that way or something. Come on. Get your mind off of the knife and start using one to eat better. We can exercise like we've been doing. Your stomach looks fine."

In today's culture it's easy for us to want to express our feelings by taking action against our bodies rather than to grieve and eventually accept our emotions. Our bodies become the outward skin for all our internal anxieties.

For Denise, life isn't going as planned. Her stomach is a distraction from the emotional pain of potentially facing the future without a man and a family. In other words, when she focuses on her stomach, she doesn't have to think about being single and unhappy about it. At the moment, that reality is overwhelming her and she is searching for a quick fix. And the bait of self-improvement tells Denise that the path to happiness is to change her body; that like the perfect ending in a movie, her new stomach will get the guy. (Of course, after her "problem" stomach is tucked, it will be something else.) If she doesn't change her thinking, she'll continue to try something fishy—expensive and faddish solutions aimed at false fulfillment.

The old bait and switch

We like distraction. I briefly mentioned this before. Distraction is one of the contemporary enemies of our souls and spiritual wellness. It pulls us away from reality and allows us to focus on the unimportant issues of life. It keeps us superficial and lets us avoid painful feelings. And maintaining an external focus on our bodies allows us to be distracted from an internal focus—one that involves our spiritual and emotional lives. If we can be distracted from emotional pain and spiritual emptiness, we can easily be hooked by body anxiety.

Years ago, psychiatrist Hilda Bruch noted in her seminal book, *Conversations with Anorexics*, that anorexics transfer their severe dissatisfaction with their lives to dissatisfaction with their bodies. Dr. Bruch claimed this resulted in their bodies being treated like something foreign that needed to be controlled and disciplined.[10] When this perspective would take over, the body became emotionally disconnected from the human soul and spirit.

What Dr. Bruch observed years ago with anorexics now rings true for most women. It seems we are treating our bodies like foreign objects—objects outside of ourselves—that constantly need correcting or fixing. In a sense, we no longer own our bodies. And our dissatisfaction with our lives may indeed be transferred to the way we feel about our bodies.

Dissatisfaction is often tied to a lack of grounding in our beliefs and not knowing who we are. Consequently, we look to things, objects, and others to define us. We think if we could be loved by another, our problems would be solved.

Like Denise, many of us believe finding a man is the solution. But this is shortsighted, because men, like our bodies, can let us down. Even the best man can't possibly give us everything we need to be secure in who we are. There is only One who can offer such completion: God.

The solution, then, is to reconnect our bodies to our souls and spirits. To realistically reconsider the meaning we give to things that matter little versus those that matter much. Denise, for example, has not considered her life through the lens of God. What does He have planned for her? Is there purpose in her being single at this time? What can she do both emotionally and spiritually to rechannel her discontent? Often, getting involved in acts of kindness, being available to others, reaching out to the needy, and helping the less fortunate are tasks that take our minds off ourselves and give meaning to our day-to-day lives.

For Denise to puncture her stomach through cosmetic surgery may lead to a temporary fix, but eventually her feelings of anxiety will return. Not because trying to fix her stomach is wrong, but because she is treating a symptom rather than the problem. Her problem is that she is spiritually dry—she is a fish out of water, disconnected from her spiritual life, and emotionally ill-equipped to deal with unfulfilled expectations. She fails to realize that God hasn't abandoned her or ignored her dreams. She has abandoned Him, feeling disappointed in the way her life is going. So she tries to fix herself and turns to the larger culture for answers to her disillusionment. She is distracted by the bait and has swallowed the hook.

Meanwhile, God waits patiently to partner with Denise and work His plans in her life. She just needs to invite Him into the process with all her heart, mind, and body. Intimacy with her Creator is needed. Less self-focus is recommended. More self-awareness in terms of dating patterns would help her make changes.

Oswald Chambers says it best in his January 22 devotional: "We will find what we are looking for if we will concentrate on Him. We get distracted from God and irritable with Him while

He continues to say to us, 'Look to Me, and be saved . . . .' Our difficulties, our trials, and our worries about tomorrow all vanish when we look to God. Wake yourself up and look to God. Build your hope on Him. No matter how many things seem to be pressing in on you, be determined to push them aside and look to Him."[11] I also like how the apostle Paul talks about this:

> Don't become so well-adjusted to your culture that you fit into it without even thinking. Instead, fix your attention on God. You'll be changed from the inside out. Readily recognize what he wants from you, and quickly respond to it. Unlike the culture around you, always dragging you down to its level of immaturity, God brings the best out of you, develops well-formed maturity in you.[12]

Unfortunately, many of us don't have the maturity Paul mentions. We don't know how to resist the cultural pull of body obsession. But the apostle doesn't leave us hanging. He tells us how to resist: we are to fix our attention on God.

According to WordReference.com, *attention* means "the work of caring for or attending to someone or something."[13] If our attention is focused on our rounded stomach, we must intentionally shift our attention to our Creator. When we do this, our lives begin to change.

The more we attend to God, the more we develop an intimacy that leads to readily recognizing what He wants from us. We realize He isn't looking for six-pack abs—instead He wants our hearts completely surrendered to Him. I briefly mentioned in another chapter that when I had a boyfriend who loved me unconditionally, I forgot about the size of my nose. This was an insight into the power of God's love in my life.

Any woman feels free in the presence of a person who loves her unconditionally. God is the One who does. When my attention is fixed on His love for me, my body insecurity fades. I am with the One who loves me completely. Flawed and imperfect, I can only see His gaze when I look into His eyes. Only then do I begin to see a clearer reflection of who I am. The truth of my real beauty is revealed.

Paul further instructs us:

> *God wants us to grow up, to know the whole truth and tell it in love—like Christ in everything. We take our lead from Christ, who is the source of everything we do. He keeps us in step with each other. His very breath and blood flow through us, nourishing us so that we will grow up healthy in God, robust in love. And so I insist—and God backs me up on this—that there be no going along with the crowd, the empty-headed, mindless crowd. They've refused for so long to deal with God that they've lost touch not only with God but with reality itself.*[14]

Have we lost touch with God and reality? It's possible to move away from His love. When we do, our spirits become dry and need reviving. However, the more we move toward God and become intimate, the more we are revived. He breathes life into us through His Word and presence.

The psalmist requests, "Create in me a clean heart, O God; and renew a right spirit within me."[15] A right spirit isn't one that wars against the body. It is one that longs for intimacy with the Giver of life.

With God's love flowing through us, we can accept our imperfect stomachs because our eyes are fixed on the One who loves us. So stop falling for the old bait and switch. Distraction carries us away from God and to other things that won't bring us happiness or control. It's time to look to the One who can help. Minimize your distractions, work through your interpersonal issues, and refocus on God. He wants to work His purposes in you, and that's a truth we can all stomach.

The Lessons

- Something's fishy. Don't fall for the culture's bait and switch.
- The only right stomach is not a flat stomach.
- Tone, don't groan!

CHAPTER 6

A Pain in the Butt

How many times have you asked a friend, "Do these jeans make my butt look fat?" Or maybe it's not the jeans but a dress or another pair of pants. Come to think of it, we don't even have to ask anyone. We just look in the mirror and assume, because it's a worry most of us have.

Ahhh, the gluteus maximus—sounds like a Greek ruler, doesn't it? Presenting your Highness (or would that be your Heinie?), Gluteus Maximus! One thing is certain: gluteus maximus does rule—not a country but our thoughts!

We forget that our posterior has a function unrelated to making us miserable. It extends our hip, moving our thigh to the rear.[1] Sounds important, doesn't it? It is. We clearly need this strong and large muscle in the body. But function isn't usually our concern.

I remember reading a quote from supermodel Elle Macpherson when she was pregnant: "The breasts go first, and then the waist, and then the butt. Nobody ever tells you that you get a butt when you get pregnant." Well, Elle, you do get a butt when you are pregnant! Booty expansion is part of the body's way of preparing for the baby and birth. To my surprise, no one ever told me that giving birth would feel like my bum was exploding! But then, giving birth for the first time is full of surprises.

When we dislike specific body parts, we lose sight of the fact that the primary function of our body parts is not to interfere with our minds, but to work together as a unit. Each part serves a function. All parts are significant. We need our glutes even if they are the butt of many jokes and a source of insecurity.

Now it's true that certain body parts are more glamorous than others. No one I know becomes particularly excited about elbows, for example. Elbows are rather neutral when you think about them. The bum, however, isn't neutral. It enjoys a rather schizo-phrenic existence. On the one hand, it's associated with passing gas and painful hemorrhoids. Many of us grew up not even being able to reference this body part without getting our mouths washed out with soap. And being called "a pain in the butt" or "butt head" isn't exactly a compliment. On the other hand (or should I say "cheek"?), the bum is a sensual area of our body asso-ciated with sexuality. Because of this, it has received a great deal of attention. And that attention has everything to do with form, not function.

Implanting a new idea

It was one of those nights when I really didn't want to watch tele-vision, but I wasn't feeling well and didn't seem to have the energy to do anything else. So I flipped on the set and didn't care what was on as long as it took my mind off of feeling sick. As I aimlessly channel surfed, I happened upon a documentary involving two women who had saved up their money for plastic surgery.

A documentary on plastic surgery is hardly an unusual topic

for TV these days. What interested me was the *kind* of plastic surgery one of the women was having—buttocks implants! Honestly, I didn't even know there was such a thing! So I sat there, glued to the glutes, fascinated by this woman's desire to increase the size of her rear.

Now I realize my naïveté was informed by the fact that I am a Caucasian female. Most white women I know are typically trying to decrease their bum sizes, not increase them. Until recently, the itty bitty booty was highly desired in white culture. My African-American and Hispanic friends, however, tell me this is a white woman's hang-up. As one woman put it, "The classic booty has been celebrated in the African-American culture for generations. . . . Long before singing superstars Beyonce and Jennifer Lopez (JLo) were on the scene, the ample booty has been the epitome of feminine beauty." Thanks to these women, the rounded, full butt is now a star. And because of that, more women, white or of color, now want this bootylicious look.

The woman in the documentary felt her bum was too small and needed more roundness in order for it to fit with her large frame. She talked about JLo's influence in her life like a religious conversion. JLo was her inspiration and the reason she consented to the surgery, although there was no indication JLo was paying for her surgery.

So there I sat, trying to appreciate this woman's desire to change her derriere while trying my best to undo years of believing the small bum was the best bum. When it came to booty, the message was now that bigger was better. Live and learn!

In the documentary, the plastic surgeon explained that he was placing implants made of a silicone shelf into this woman's buttocks. These were designed to look natural and give her a more rounded appearance. Then the surgical risks were reviewed: implants can cause infection, bleeding, and can shift, producing an asymmetrical look. They can also tear, rupture, or break. And if you have the incision for the implants in the gluteal crease, the rate of infection is higher than having the incision at the bottom of the cheeks (OK, this was more than I wanted to know!). Like real estate, location matters.

The operation was performed under general anesthesia and took about three hours. The incision was made down the buttock crease in order to hide the scars. Cutting makes me a little queasy. And cutting in the gluteal crease, well . . . let's just say I had to close my eyes for a few seconds when the slicing began. Though I may have missed something, a sort of pocket was made in which to place the implant. In this case, the implants were positioned under the *gluteus maximus* muscle, high enough so that they were above the area she would use to sit. Thank goodness, because I can't imagine trying to sit on those silicone shelves!

After both cheeks were finished, the woman was stitched up and sent to recovery. About three hours later she was on her way home and ordered not to sit for about ten days and to do very little for the next month. At this point she didn't look too happy. In fact, she looked like she was in incredible pain.

Of course we meet her again months later, when she is thrilled with her new look and finally has the booty she's always wanted. No longer bummed with her ordeal (sorry, I couldn't resist), she was extolling the virtues of the bigger, rounded bottom. She did mention that the implants weren't as soft as she'd imagined, and they had a more unnatural feel to them than she expected. However, she was convinced the entire experience was worth her time, money, and the risk. All I can say is this surgery gives new meaning to the phrase "a pain in the butt"! Invited pain is not a guest I want around.

I noticed that as I was watching (or more like peeking) when the incisions were being made, I had unconsiously placed my hand on my own bum as an act of empathy. Yes, I know this woman was under general anesthesia, but having that part of the body cut just can't be too pleasant. I couldn't imagine going deep under the skin to place the implants. My only point of reference was getting a shot in the butt, and this was definitely more complicated than that. Better her than me.

Interestingly, this woman wasn't alone in her quest for the perfect derriere. Buttock implant surgery is gaining popularity, especially among women.[2] The American Society for Aesthetic Plastic Surgery reported a 533 percent increase in buttock implant surgeries between 2002 and 2003. They divided the women seeking this surgery into two main groups.

One group is younger women who want to have a more curvaceous figure like Hollywood's superstars. The other group is comprised of older women trying to regain a more youthful look. When the booty begins to sag and go flat, the claim is that buttock implants can bring back a younger appearance.

This interest in the curvaceous bum doesn't stop there either. Commercials are singing the praises of the bigger booty. Take the Nike ad campaign, "Big Butts and Thunder Thighs," that asks the question, "What story does your body tell?" (Read this book and you'll know!) The ad features a close-up of a big, round, muscular bum with the tagline:

> My Butt is big and round like the letter C, and 10,000 lunges have made it rounder but not smaller. And that's just fine. It's a space heater for my side of the bed. It's my ambassador. To those who walk behind me, it's a border collie that herds skinny women away from the best deals at clothing sales. My butt is big and that's just fine. And those who might scorn it are invited to kiss it. Just do it.[3]

While I applaud Nike for using models that aren't stick-thin and for writing ad copy that celebrates a larger backside (although they could have left out the invitation to kiss it), I still have a problem with the ad. The Nike bum doesn't represent the average woman any better than the barely existent bum of model Kate Moss.

Nike caters to athletic women, so the ad is geared to that demographic. However, the amount of working out you'd have to do to achieve the look presented in the ad is again beyond most of us. Even if I did the Buns of Steel workout or jumped on the butt blaster machine at the gym every day, my back end would never look like the one in this ad. What story does my body tell? Not this one! The ad shows the body of someone incredibly muscular and fit and athletic, and born with just the right amount of padding. Not the bum of ordinary folk like me.

Nevertheless, enhanced derierres are showing up in department stores as well. The next time you shop in the women's clothing section, take a look at the bum on the mannequin. In fact, walk behind her and grab a cheek. You might notice that the mannequin (still a size four) has a bigger and rounder bum.

You also might guess that with all this attention to bootys, booty e-mail questions and chats are popping up more frequently on many Web sites and blogs. One teen asked if having sex could increase her size back there! I wanted to say, "Honey, let's consider a little counseling. Using sex as a means to an end of having a better body . . . how about thinking about the risks of sexual contact versus the way your body might look!"

Maybe you are thinking this emphasis on the bigger booty is great—finally we are losing the emaciated model look. Well, don't be fooled. It doesn't signal the acceptance of larger women at all. If that was the case, I'd be shaking my booty with you. In reality, *all this signals is the remaking of an ideal.* The bum is just another body part redesigned and objectified in order to fit someone's idea of feminine perfection.

For those of you who have a naturally rounded bigger booty, you are the current target of big business in advertisement. *Carpe diem!* The rest of us are supposed to wrestle with the notion that we don't measure up to the current cultural ideal. Again, this is an opportunity to feel inadequate. That is, if you let it be so. I suggest you don't.

What lies beneath

Ah, but there is more to this bum story. Not only do we want a well-rounded booty, but we also want one that is smooth and contoured. Dimples on facial cheeks are cute; dimples on the rear cheeks are not! It's what lies beneath the skin's surface that leaves us bummed out! It's got a name, it ain't pretty, and about 85 percent of us will develop it.[4] Called cellulite, it is my longtime companion.

Even though my first encounter with cellulite was on my thigh, we all know that cellulite is not confined to one body part. It can be found on the inner knees, hips, lower abdomen, and under the arms. All too often, though, those puckering dimples appear on our bums as well. Even supermodel Tyra Banks admits she has cellulite. Because of air-brushing, lighting, computer altering, and other techniques aimed at giving us a perfect image of her, what lies beneath is simply hidden. But it's there.

Although we treat cellulite like a disease, it isn't. It doesn't come from toxic buildup or inflammation, as many of the product advertisers would like you to believe. No, it involves genetics, hormones, and anatomy. It has to do with fat structures beneath the skin and connective tissue. Simply put, cellulite is fat that is deposited in pockets below the surface of the skin. This fat pushes through the connective tissue that is responsible for distributing the fat evenly, causing the surface of our skin to ripple.

This cottage cheese look is an equal-opportunity annoyance

for most of us. Just one more reason to be dissatisfied with our bums. However, the extra fat under the surface does serve a function. It is our body's natural way of storing extra calories that may be needed for pregnancy and nursing. The problem seems to be when the connective tissue doesn't do its job properly or loses its elasticity. Then the fat isn't evenly distributed and the surface of our skin gets that orange-peel look.

I hesitate to add this because I know how easy it is to blame our mothers for most everything, but cellulite is genetic. This skin structure is passed down from mother to daughter. It's like inheriting a piece of jewelry you really hate. Visible or displayed, it's part of your family history.

There are several reasons why women have more cellulite than men. Overall, women have more body fat than men. Also, men have a different structure of connective tissue that doesn't lend as easily to the development of fat pockets. How nice for them!

In addition, cellulite can develop with the surge of hormones at puberty or pregnancy; women tend to store fat in the lower parts of their bodies due to the way estrogen is produced. Men also have thicker skin, which tends to hide the rippling effect better than women's thinner skin. For once, we have something thinner than men and it doesn't work to our advantage. Go figure!

Dieting is one of our attempts to lose the dimply stuff. When we lose weight, we do lose a proportion of the cellulite fat through shrinkage, but it doesn't magically disappear. With weight loss, the skin adapts. Collagen and elastic fibers retract, but they do their best work before the age of thirty-five or forty.[5] So for those of us at midlife, we've got physiology working against us. As collagen and elastic fibers in the skin age and weaken, the dimpling seems to worsen.

Because we don't find cellulite glamorous, we go to tremendous lengths to rid ourselves of these dimples. There are so many "treatments" that you could spend your life savings just addressing this one body issue. And I have to admit, I have a favorite solution: the invention of the anticellulite jeans! Released by an Italian clothing designer, this is a truly innovative product. Yes, you read that correctly. Anticellulite jeans!

When these jeans were introduced, you purchased a pair saturated with anticellulite cream for $139. In the lining of the jeans were microcapsules of retinol and chitosan, which are combined to make something called Skintex. This cream is supposed to stimulate collagen and thus reduce cellulite. When you wear the jeans, the friction between your body and the jeans releases the cream, which is then absorbed into your body! According to the manufacturers, you would get about thirty to fifty washings per pair.[6]

Now if you are excited by this novel approach, please know that dermotologists are not![7] Don't start Googling anticellulite jeans for purchase! They're clever, but not exactly the fat melter they were designed to be.

Of course there are more creams too. Lots of creams. Expensive creams. When it comes to slathering yourself with expensive products, Dr. Lisa Donofrio, associate clinical professor of dermatology at Yale University, has this to say. It sums up the position most physicians take on the effectiveness of lotions and potions: "Expecting a topical cream to 'soak into' the fat is kind of like placing a sandwich on your belly and expecting it to 'soak into' your stomach. The cream will never get near the fat deposits."[8]

When you talk with doctors or scientists, most will tell you that the preponderance of "cures" out there are bogus. The best you can do is temporaily alter your appearance with various products, lights, and massages, or experiment with new treatments. Be careful though. Many of these "treatments" are expensive, need to be repeated, can be painful, have risks and side effects, and need more study. And when you find something that provides a slight benefit to appearance, you have to continue doing whatever you did to keep the small gain.

Contrary to popular belief, liposuction isn't recommended for cellulite reduction and may make the dimpling worse. Liposuction is designed to get at deep fat, and cellulite is too close to the surface to be helped by it. And remember that those fibrous bands have everything to do with the ripple look. Cellulite is a skin problem, not a fat one.[9]

Since it is what lies beneath the skin that really causes cellulite, developing an effective treatment is challenging. Let's give high marks to the Italian denim designers when it comes to creativity. But creativity is not how we measure success. Results matter.

The issue with cellulite is that we don't like what we see. However, what we see doesn't represent the complete picture or the depth of the problem. Because of this, cellulite is a good example of a deeper truth. Trying to change our outward appearance without accounting for the internal breakdown won't bring lasting change whether we are talking cellulite or a sagging booty. It is what takes place in the deep interior of our being that matters. If we hate what we see, if it looks too dimply and ugly, if the mistakes of the past keep breaking through to the surface, we need spiritual liposuction. Or better yet, since we are talking bootys, we need a spiritual enema. As gross as that may sound, sometimes a deep cleansing is needed to release all the junk of our pasts.

Too many of us are constipated by guilt, unable to move efficiently in the life God has for us. We feel blocked, loaded down with the mistakes of our pasts, and unable to let go. Well, it's time to stop sitting on our rear ends—we need to lose that unhealthy guilt.

If you've confessed your past mistakes, repented of wrong decisions and choices, and asked God to take the waste of your life, it's gone. Flushed away. You are new and cleansed and need to stop condemning yourself. God does not condemn you. He only sees you clean and restored to spiritual health. Accept His forgiveness. It came with a tremendous price and yet is offered freely. All you have to do is accept it.

And while you are flushing out unhealthy guilt, flush away the toxin of shame. It does nothing but increase your feelings of inadequacy. Shame says you are flawed. It is a pain in the butt with no good purpose.

To get rid of it, first think about why you feel shame. Most likely, your feeling is based on a lie. Identify that lie. Once you've identified the lie, ask God to speak His truth to your spirit. Revelation and experience of His truth bring healing. Then forgive anyone who caused you to feel shame. Release that person to God and be free from the power of shame.

If you continue to feel inadequate about your dimpled bum after you release the guilt and shame from your life, ask God if He can still use you to do good on this earth despite your back end. I hope you feel a little silly (though not shamed) doing this.

Of course His answer will be that He can use you, bitty or bodacious booty. It's so irrelevant to the larger picture. He's not waiting for you to acquire the perfect body. But He does want you to get rid of the wasted years and toxins. And His promise is that if you release it all to Him, He will restore what was lost, fix what was broken, and make new those things that lie beneath. Then, whenever anyone tries to make you relive the past, turn to that person and say, "But God says . . . ," and remember, you are free and clean.

The Lessons

- It's a pain in the butt to alter your butt!
- Shame and unhealthy guilt are toxins that need to be flushed away.
- Beneath the shame and guilt are lies. Swap the lies for the truth and be free!

CHAPTER 7

An About Face

The other day my kids and I were browsing through some of my old yearbooks. They about fell over when they saw my pictures. Not that I blamed them; these were the days before girls wore makeup for school pictures. Yes, I am *that* old.

So there I was: my albino skin with freckles (which do show up in black and white), looking washed out and featureless, leaving me wondering why any guy ever gave me a first glance. "I'm just not very photogenic!" I used to say. By the reaction of my kids, I could see this was an understatement. However, my children are kind souls who love their mom. Their comment was, "Mom, you look a lot better now." Hey, there are some benefits to aging!

As we closed the pages of my school days, I felt it was necessary to follow up this brief trek down memory lane with a short discussion about beauty. I wanted my kids to remember that beauty is more than a pretty face on a page. It is something that radiates from within. It is seen through our countenance—

the way we carry ourselves and the confidence we have in who we are.

Looking at those old pictures, I tried to remember how I felt about myself during those younger days. It seemed that my body image changed as often as my hairstyle. The years I felt more secure, the pictures were better. You could see the confidence in my eyes. Even though "stunning" or "beautiful" were not labels I ever heard, I was more accepting of who I was when things were going well in my life. The problem with this is that when things weren't going so well, I lost my grounding. The insecurities returned.

If you think about the women who typically fit our description of stunning—Elizabeth Taylor, Sophia Loren, or, in more recent years, Halle Berry, Angelina Jolie, Tyra Banks, or Julia Roberts—it's interesting that the faces we rate as beautiful tend to be symmetrical. From the inner to outer corners of the eyes, to the jawbone, cheeks, and outer edges of the nostrils, researchers agree that symmetry on the face influences our perceptions of beauty. Perhaps that explains why so many people try to alter their faces. They want that symmetry we find so attractive.

Facing reality

Meet Sha. She is nineteen years old and was raised in Texas. Her ambition in life is not only to have a beautiful face but a famous one. Sha idolizes actress Pamela Anderson and thinks she is beautiful. Anderson is her role model for physical beauty and success. In order to achieve her goals of recreating herself into a Pamela Anderson clone, Sha became a "patient" on MTV's television show, *I Want a Famous Face*.

In case you've never seen this program, the concept of the show is this: Fans of famous people like Brad Pitt, Jennifer Lopez, Julia Roberts, Britney Spears, and yes, Pamela Anderson, undergo cosmetic surgery in order to look more like their idols. The desired transformation is documented by television cameras as viewers witness young people doing whatever is physically necessary to create a look similar to the stars they adore. The more they can approximate the look of their idols, the better. The body-altering procedures shown have included facial and breast implants, lip augmentation, gastric bypass surgery, and even transsexual hormone therapy.

After undergoing breast and lip implants and liposuction under her chin, Sha reported feeling very satisfied with the outcome. Not only did Sha feel more beautiful, but she looked more like the woman she wanted to be—Pamela Anderson.

Reality television allows us to witness the transformation of many women from plain Janes to beauties. Perhaps you watched twenty-eight-year-old Kelly and twenty-seven-year-old Rachel compete in a beauty contest after having serious plastic surgery, exercise sessions, and "psychological treatment" aimed at transforming them from "ugly ducklings" into "beautiful swans." In the latest installment of reality television, *The Swan*, we followed both girls being physically altered with the purpose of entering them in a beauty contest to compete with other beautiful faces. Not exactly the Purpose Driven Life!

Of course, there is the mother lode of both these programs, *Extreme Makeover*—the show that brought plastic surgery into our living rooms and exposed more of us to the possibility of changing our faces. The basic premise of this show is to have people talk about all the things they don't like about their bodies and then undergo cosmetic surgery and other beauty-enhancing sessions in order to correct those "problems." In every show, major changes to the face are requested.

The message of all these shows is this: If you don't like your looks, you can change them. Apparently twelve million people agree, since every year that many people have plastic surgery.[1] Please understand that with all my focus on cosmetic surgery, I am not totally opposed to it. If you are someone who has had cosmetic surgery and feel better about your life, I am not here to condemn you. My concern has to do with *why* we are altering our looks at such record rates and how these shows feed off the negative body image perceptions so many of us already have. And rarely do we see the reality of surgery—the risks, the failures, the cost, the maintenance required, etc.—in these supposed "reality" shows.

Face up to it

One of the most recent trends in facial help is Botox injections. Botox, in case you don't know, is a toxin that, when injected into the forehead, temporarily relaxes the muscle (it actually paralyzes it) and decreases the frown lines associated with aging and sun damage. The effects from the injections typically last about three to six months.

Due to the popularity of Botox injections, we now have Botox parties, where someone decides to invite several of her friends to her home, along with a plastic surgeon. Once everyone arrives, you enjoy lunch or a social time. The surgeon brings enough Botox for the entire group and, for a reduced price, can inject several women at one setting. In other words, you eat, mingle, and smooth out your forehead all at the same time!

I have a friend, a sensible and wonderful friend, who did Botox. In her case, it worked like a charm and she had no side effects. She's not image-obsessed and has the sweetest character. Honestly, I didn't worry that she was turning into a body-obsesser. Personally, though, I question whether or not it's a good idea to have poison injected that close to my brain! And do I want to have lunch with a toxin? I'm taking a pass for now.

Of course, Botox isn't the only way we can alter our faces

these days. We have
the making even a
surgery, facelifts,
mentation, fore
chemical pee
hyaluronic ac

Are you
of these don
and smile—b
frowning, because you
You don't have to do any or
are out there, ready for our consump
to participate.

While most of us probably won't opt for a facelin.
ticipate to some degree in this frenzy to beautify our faces.
many of us have had chemical peels or even have our own mini-
dermabrasion machines in our homes? I have one, although I've
yet to use it. But I will. Or what about those teeth-whitening
strips? And there are makeup, facials, and other face and skin
products. I've got drawers full of these products, but facial beauty
takes a lot of work and is expensive! My problem is I don't have
time for it!

I have another question related to this. I honestly don't know
how it takes women hours to "put on their face." I've tried it, but
I'm finished in ten minutes and don't know what else to do. What
is it that takes so long? E-mail me with your answers, please.

Let's face it, though. We see no problem with dermabrasion,
chemical peels, or teeth whitening, although cutting and res-
culpting may make us a bit more uneasy. And these surgical inter-
ventions should, since they have more risks. That said, all surgical
and non-surgical efforts are geared toward the same goal: keeping
our faces looking younger and fresher. And ten years from now,

hat we might do, given the current tech-
face and skin care.

es to look good. It's one of the reasons we
y makeup and do our hair. The face is often the
hat we call beautiful. We should attend to look-
ow far we go has to do with what motivates us and
e trying to accomplish.

lip service

king of our faces, one of our most sensual zones is our lips.
ps inspire poetry, movies, and even love. The biblical King
olomon's bride shares these thoughts during her courtship,
"May he kiss me with the kisses of his mouth."[2]

Lips are frequently mentioned in one of my favorite Shake-
spearean plays, *Romeo and Juliet.* Romeo discovers his new love,
Juliet, at a masquerade ball. He is so taken by her beauty that he
tells her, "My lips, two blushing pilgrims, ready stand to smooth
that rough touch with a tender kiss."[3] After a witty dialogue
about lips and sin, they kiss and are smitten.

Later, when Romeo finds Juliet asleep in the tomb and mistakes her drug-induced state for death, he laments, "Death, that
has sucked the honey of thy breath, hath no power yet upon thy
beauty. Thou art not conquered. Beauty's ensign yet is crimson in
thy lips and in thy cheeks, and death's pale flag is not advanced
there."[4]

I admit I'm a sucker for this type of dialogue. Lips have always
been a source of sensuality. Now, more than ever, sensual lips are
defined as full, pouty, and voluptuous. Unfortunately, this means
most of us will fail the "lips must-have" test in terms of meeting
the current ideal. Thick, full lips are typically genetic. Even if you
are fortunate enough to have full lips, they thin as we age (and
smoke) because the tissue in them diminishes.

Nevertheless, if you want "the look," there are several paths possible. One option is to have collagen injected into your lips, or you can go for a permanent look with lip implants. Lip implants use threads of a foam-like material to make the lips look larger, but that material sometimes cannot be removed because the lip tissue grows around the implant. There is also a risk of infection and migration of the implants.

Another option is to have fat taken from your own buttocks or tummy and injected into your lips! I guess this kills two birds with one stone! However, be aware: Over time, the fat can reabsorb and deflate the lips.[5] Of course, some of us feel there is a never-ending supply!

I am not recommending these procedures, just explaining why we suddenly have so many people who look like they have a permanent pucker. If you're like me—frightened by the idea of anyone putting a syringe in your lip or implanting a foreign object that could leave you with a crooked smile—you may be wondering about the over two-hundred new products designed to give you full and sensual lips. Please, don't get too excited. Most of them don't do much.

Some of these products do have natural ingredients like cinnamon, peppermint, or caffeine in them that work to dilate blood vessels and cause swelling for a little while. Other products can cause burns and mouth sores, so you have to be careful with experimenting.[6] My guess is that a plate full of hot wings sprinkled with habanero peppers could give you the pucker you want with a lot less time, trouble, and cost!

Even if we don't augment or enhance our lips, we are always soothing them with balms, sunscreens, and lipsticks. We drink bottles of water and refrain from picking or licking our lips in order to prevent dryness. We want them moist and full, even if our genetic constitution says otherwise.

The more we promote full lips in the media and among celebrities as the look *du jour*, the more they become just another body part ready for a remake. And with them comes another opportunity to feel dissatisfied with how we look. Oscar Wilde once said, "Most people are other people. Their thoughts are someone else's opinions, their lives a mimicry, their passions a quotation." What truth there is in these words today! Help us all not to fall prey to trying to be other people. I don't want a famous face or to lose face. Let's celebrate our uniqueness, not our conformity. Let's not allow insecurity to rule our lives.

Comparing lipsticks

Have you ever attended one of those women's events where they make you empty your purse and take out your lipstick? As you hold the lipstick in your hand and turn the casing to reveal an inch of the tube, the speaker begins to give you a lipstick personality lesson. Depending on the shape of your lipstick—if it slants, is concave, has a curved tip, has a rounded top, flat top, or sharp angle on one side or both—you are assigned certain personality traits.

According to this less-than-scientific test, I am someone who abides by rules, is a great follower, doesn't like too much attention, is reserved, and likes to color my hair. All of that was gathered from the shape of my lipstick! Not exactly based on hard science, it was no surprise to me that my lipstick told lies. If the truth be known, it was dead wrong! However, I had a good laugh pretending my lipstick had personality oozing out of it.

Lipsticks don't help us figure out who we are, and neither do other people—unless, of course, they are counselors or someone designated to help us figure out our life. So stop comparing yourself to other people. Stop lamenting that you don't have the lips of Angelina Jolie. Stop biting your skinny upper lip. Stop wishing your lipstick had a flat top and was concave so you could be a great detective and live a complex and exciting life (hey, that's what the lipstick personality test says!). In other words, *stop* chomping at the bit to be someone else.

No good purpose is served in negatively comparing our faces to the faces of others, famous or not. Comparisons only bring feelings of inadequacy and low esteem. Comparing ourselves to others works against celebrating our individuality. And in a day and age when we are desperate to find our unique selves within the mass of humanity, comparisons only make matters worse.

As teenagers, we constantly compared our bodies to others, but hopefully, as we mature, we see the futility and let go of this unhealthy behavior. I'll be the first to admit that letting go doesn't happen naturally. We have to work at it as we become more comfortable in our own skin. And part of our maturity is recognizing the principle of individuality that operates in our lives. In the same way that no two snowflakes are alike, neither are we. Each of us reveals a glimpse of God's incredible diversity. While there is great emphasis in our culture on celebrating diversity, we lag seriously behind in the area of body image.

Popular teacher Beth Moore addresses this tendency to compare as it relates to insecurity. She points out that we always seem to want the blessings of someone else. Instead of focusing on how we've been blessed and what our own strengths and talents are, we look to others and want what they have. Doing this brings great insecurity . . . because we are not living our lives in the unique blessings God has given us. We constantly think we fall short because we compare what we have with others. Living in this type of insecurity creates emotional bondage.

When you find yourself making a negative comparison about yourself to someone else, stop and think about your individuality and how boring the world would be if we all looked and acted alike. Make a list of your unique strengths and keep it by your bed. Review it when you start thinking the hair is blonder on the other side.

The human face is wonderfully unique. So much so that infants are highly sensitive to the structure and shape of our faces long before they discriminate by our bodies.[7] That's why a sixteen-month-old can grab your leg and think you are her mom when you aren't. A baby needs to see that familiar face to know her mom has been found. And if she sees the face and it's not her mom's, lack of recognition can bring sheer terror.

Perhaps when it comes to accepting our faces, it's a matter of degree. I'm not telling you to discard your makeup or cancel your spa appointment. Roll out your micro-dermabrasion and use it regularly if that's what you want to do. I'm all for looking good, and I certainly wear makeup and believe it improves my appearance. But the question remains, how far are we willing to go to achieve a certain look?

Assessing our motives for altering our appearance is important, especially as more cosmetic procedures become less expensive and available to the masses. We have more and more options that require more and more expense that can lead to more and more obsession. Where do we stop? Studies show that if you want to change one aspect of your body but feel generally happy with your overall appearance, you will do better with a cosmetic procedure than someone who expects radical changes from surgeries.[8]

This is why the reality TV shows mentioned previously are cause for concern. The expectations of a new life, new opportunities, improved esteem, and boosted confidence don't happen when other life issues are involved. Most likely, other life issues *are* involved, based on the stories of the people who participate in these shows. When we look to face-altering procedures to bring new opportunities and esteem and to boost our moods, maybe we aren't addressing the true root of the problem. So what are those other issues?

The need to accommodate others can be one motive. If you are someone who wants to please another person by changing your looks, think again. Accommodating another person's idea of beauty is not a good idea. If that person changes his or her view of beauty, becomes critical, or leaves you, what then? You've basically handed your self-worth on a platter to another person to serve up when and how he or she pleases.

If you want to make alterations because you think the rest of your life will fall in place with the changes, forget it. You are being naïve and only putting a bandage on a deeper problem. You might look better, but you haven't addressed the discontent that lies beneath the surface, as we discussed in the previous chapter.

If you are a perfectionist, you might seek surgeries and procedures in an attempt to sculpt a perfect face. Don't go there. It won't correct your perfectionistic tendencies. You won't be satisfied. Cosmetic surgery for this reason is not a good choice.

If you are a plastic surgery addict or have a body image disorder or eating disorder, you need counseling, not surgery. For example, I worked with a woman who had more than twelve cosmetic surgeries as a way to deal with the rejection she felt from men. None of the surgeries ever corrected her low esteem or took away the hurt of those rejections. If your body image problems are caused by issues like abuse, criticism, rejection, and other psychological wounds, you won't heal those wounds by going under the knife or doing a chemical peel. I wish it were that simple, but it isn't.

The root of body dissatisfaction has to do with esteem, confidence, and psychological well-being.[9] So it is very important to ask yourself why you want to make changes. In some cases, plastic surgery can even make the root issues worse.[10] It's one thing to want to improve your appearance, to cover scars, or to reconstruct a facial defect, and another thing to alter your face to look like someone else. This pressure to remake ourselves into someone we are not signals unhappiness with who we are.

Do you know who you are and do you have confidence in that identity?

Faced with reality

Psychiatrist Viktor Frankl in *Man's Search for Meaning* reminds us that everything can be taken away from man except for the human freedom to choose our attitudes in any given circumstance and choose our own way.[11] He goes on to tell us that every day, every hour, every minute we have the power to make a decision to not submit to those powers that destroy the self. We have an inner freedom.

That freedom is the ability to choose. You can choose to stop obsessing and being driven by outside forces. You can choose to attend to inner forces that will change your attitudes and life in a positive direction. You have that freedom. Sometimes we make choices by being passive and doing nothing to challenge our thinking or change our lives. We just go along with the status quo. Considering the number of messages and images we encounter daily to become someone we are not, we have to actively choose to be our genuine selves.

The founder of Gestalt Therapy, psychoanalyst Fritz Perls, asks this question, "If I am what I have, and I lose what I have, who am I?" This is a profound question concerning identity. If we are no more than a beautiful face and we lose that (and we will), then who are we?

In that case, what happens when the body gives way to aging and change? Will we accept this gracefully, or will we fight it every step of the way? And what about the fact that our bodies will someday return to the dust from which they were created? Then what?

I have a friend who believes that when we die, that's the end. I find her belief incredibly depressing. It reminds me of the way the famous physician Sigmund Freud approached death. Death of the physical body, Freud believed, was equal to extinction, and so he obsessed over death and feared it tremendously. At the end of his life, when the lip cancer he fought was aggressively winning the physical battle, Freud chose to read a novel in which the hero dies in a frantic state of fear. Not exactly the most comforting choice of reading when you are facing death. The next day, Freud was euthanized by a physician friend, believing death was his final destiny.

Freud, a brilliant thinker, was unable to accept the concept of a personal God whose image he reflected. Instead he distorted that image and believed religion was an illusion for the weak. He chose to make science his god. Facing death, there was no comfort in this and no hope for eternity.

I choose to believe that when Jesus was crucified and rose again from the dead, death was conquered and we were put in right standing with God. I believe the physical body is the earthly home of the spiritual self. Death is not the end of us. Our spirits live on. If you choose to believe this, then it means that we are more than just our physical bodies. Death becomes the means to deliver us from one world to the next. This, to me, is hopeful and gives a different perspective on the importance of the body.

It also means that who we are must be built on something more than physical features, something that will last as our bodies age and weaken, something that will bring a true peace and confidence even when parts of our bodies begin to shift and fall.

For too many years I had no idea how to do this, despite being raised in the church. I struggled with identity, and so did many of my friends. One looked for her sense of self in beauty contests and popularity. Another gave in to identity confusion and got high to avoid the emptiness of not knowing who she was. Still another thought that being loved by a man would give her a sense of herself. Others, like me, tried to find that identity in scholarship and accomplishment. Yet none of this worked.

When I turned to God out of confusion and disappointment, He was right there waiting for me, ready to teach me through the Scriptures. Once I started reading my Bible, I realized God had a great deal to say about me; I just had never bothered to read much of it. I had relied on other people to give me my sense of self. Now, instead of comparing myself to others and falling short, I learned who God said I was. It wasn't about comparison at all.

Identity is developed through identification with someone. It begins with our parents and incorporates others with whom we feel an affinity. It may be a teacher, an actor, a schoolmate, or someone else who influences us positively or negatively. Some of us, like Freud, never learn to identify with our Father, God. As a result, we look to others to give us that sense of self that is so deeply desired. But others may disappoint or leave us. Not so with God. His promise is to never leave or forsake us. And while we try to idealize others and make them into the perfect people we'd like them to be, this doesn't work. In the long run, the choice is despair or God.

To me, the choice is easy. Who can compare to God? He challenges us by saying,

> So to whom will you compare me, the Incomparable? Can you picture me without reducing me? . . . "So—who is like me? Who holds a candle to me?" says The Holy. Look at the night skies: Who do you think made all this? Who marches this army of

stars out each night, counts them off, calls each by name—so magnificent! so powerful!—and never overlooks a single one?[12]

The issue is this: Who will you choose as your source of identification? God compares you to no one because He uniquely made you. In His eyes, your face reflects an aspect of His glory. He offers Himself as a way out of our insecurities. What we need, He provides. We need God to be big to handle our problems—He is. We need God to be personal, intimate, and caring—He is. Most of all, we need God to accept us, validate us as His creation, and love us flaws and all. He does.

Romans 8:29 reassures us that "God knew what he was doing from the very beginning. He decided from the outset to shape the lives of those who love him along the same lines as the life of his Son. The Son stands first in the line of humanity he restored. We see the original and intended shape of our lives there in him."

If we love God, He promises to help shape our lives and restore us. Jesus is our model, and He's hardly a conformist. True to self, Jesus never denies who He is—humble, approachable, compassionate, intimate, a champion of the poor and disenfranchised, and, most of all, the Son of God, the image of the invisible God.

It is so interesting that we don't really know what Christ looked like while He was here on earth. There is only one reference to His physical appearance that I know of in the Bible. It is found in a prophecy written hundreds of years before His birth. It reads like this,

The servant grew up before God—a scrawny seedling, a scrubby plant in a parched field. There was nothing attractive about him, nothing to cause us to take a second look. He was looked down on and passed over, a man who suffered, who knew pain firsthand. One look at him and people turned away. We looked down on him, thought he was scum.[13]

Wow. Jesus' appearance would garner little attention in today's culture. He'd be a candidate for an extreme makeover. We would prefer Jesus to have been described as tall, dark, and handsome, yet according to this reading there was nothing physically attractive about Him. He was looked down on and passed over. I wonder if this was so we wouldn't make an idol out of His appearance and miss His true identity and His purpose for coming to earth.

Jesus did not come as Adonis but *Adonai*. He did not draw crowds because He was drop-dead gorgeous. People were drawn to Him because of who He was—God's only begotten Son. Son of God and Son of man. He announces over and over that He and the Father are one. In His mind, there is no question regarding His identity. And we share in this identity when we become one of His.

If you are at all unsure of how God thinks of you and the identity you have been given, read this treasure from the book of Ephesians, "Long before he laid down earth's foundations, he had us in mind, had settled on us as the focus of his love, to be made whole and holy by his love. Long, long ago he decided to adopt us into his family through Jesus Christ. (What pleasure he took in planning this!)"[14] Reread that Scripture and insert your name in the appropriate places.

We are the focus of His love. He has had us in mind from the beginning. He knows our every hair, wrinkle, and care:

> *What marvelous love the Father has extended to us! Just look at it—we're called children of God! That's who we really are. But that's also why the world doesn't recognize us or take us seriously, because it has no idea who he is or what he's up to.*[15]

> *God's Spirit touches our spirits and confirms who we really are. We know who he is, and we know who we are: Father and children.*[16]

People who decide not to choose God will never understand this and will struggle to find their true selves. It is God's Spirit in us that tells us who we really are. It is the Spirit of Truth, and it counters insecurity. Appearance is only what we look like. *It does not define us.* To God, my face is beautiful because it reflects His image. So when I struggle with feeling inferior based on my outward appearance, I am reminded again by Paul of Tarsus's words—"When I am weak or insecure, then I am strong because God's power is working in me." God uses my imperfect face to reflect the face of God. He uses my smile to show compassion and care. Through me, the radiance of God's love can shine.

What kind of an amazing God would do this? Only one that sees us as the object of His affection:

> *All of us! Nothing between us and God, our faces shining with the brightness of his face. And so we are transfigured much like the Messiah, our lives gradually becoming brighter and more beautiful as God enters our lives and we become like him.*[17]

The living, personal, and present God wants to meet you face to face. When He does, you'll do an about-face, realizing that the transformation of the heart is reflected on the face. It is a glorious face-lift, and free of charge since the price has already been paid! My prayer is that God will mark each of our faces with His grace and glory.

The Lessons

- Stop comparing. It only brings insecurity.
- Stop trying to become someone else and enjoy being you.

PART TWO

Loosening the Grip

CHAPTER 8

Just Five More Pounds!

*I burned sixty calories. That should take care of a
peanut I had in 1962.*

—RITA RUDNER

Raise your hand if you

- have ever lied about your weight on your driver's license.
- purposely wear light clothing to your "weigh-ins" at the doctor's office.
- get depressed trying on a bathing suit.
- feel you need to lose weight.

If you are like me, your hand went up and down so many times a moment ago, you probably worked off ten calories just being truthful! (Here's a free tip: Schedule your yearly physical in the summer. Winter clothing weighs more.) It doesn't matter what we weigh. Whatever the number, we always need it to be lower. *Just five more pounds!*

As much as we hope to eventually get off the dieting roller coaster, we seem to stay on it for life. I can't say we enjoy the ups and downs, but dieting sure gives us a thrill now and then. If we lose a few pounds, we are exhilarated. But when we gain the weight back—or worse, put on more pounds—body satisfaction takes a dive into despair. Then we take a deep breath and get on track again. This time we will be successful and lose that five pounds and feel good about ourselves.

And so it goes throughout our lives, up and down. From the womb to the tomb, weight acceptance has become more than a developmental task for most of us—it's a lifelong journey. And for some who develop eating disorders, the journey is treacherous and can lead to early death.

I've often wondered if our national weight obsession is a complete distraction from truly important issues. You know how Dr. Phil McGraw asks the people on his show: "How's that working for you?" Well, I've figured out that weight obsession serves a great purpose: it keeps us focused on products and activities— things we can control to some extent—rather than people. People are always more difficult to deal with than things. And that reality can be unpleasant and certainly un-American.

OK, so maybe I sound a little like a conspiracy theorist here, but it does feel like the entire country is weight obsessed and that we have all bought in big-time. There are just too many women like myself who are not overweight but still feel like we've got to lose weight. "Just five more pounds." It's become our feminine mantra. Chant it with me, "Five more pounds, five more pounds." No, not "Four more years." Instead it's "Five more pounds." That's right. You've got it. The problem is that when we lose the "five more pounds," there is always another five more to go. We can't win!

Personally, two of my biggest obstacles are that I like to eat and I like food. The double whammy! Food and eating are sacrosanct in my German-Hungarian family. All my aunts and my mom are fabulous cooks and should have opened their own Babushka Bakery when I was growing up. I could have bought stock . . . we would be a major franchise today!

Aunt Betty is known for her homemade cinnamon rolls, Aunt Ruth for her fudgy brownies, Aunt Mart for her banana cream pie, and my mom for her cherry pie slicer—a pie-like delight you can only make with fresh-picked sour cherries from the Midwest that has a thin icing on top. My mouth is watering just thinking about it. And these foods are just the top vote-getters.

Food not only took center stage in my American-German household, but it was serious business . . . and competitive. For years, my mom tried to duplicate Aunt Mart's banana cream pie, only to discover that Aunt Mart purposely left out one important ingredient in the written recipe. No wonder no one could duplicate it!

Food was so important that family get-togethers were basically food floods. We always had at least five or six desserts, two or three creamed vegetables (I was an adult before I knew vegetables could be steamed), two meat choices, homemade rolls, and all kinds of other goodies. Weddings were judged successful based on the size of the meal. If you decided to have only punch and cake at the reception, it was better not to marry into the family at all, because you'd never live it down.

Despite all this incredible emphasis on eating and food, I grew up a normal-weight child and teen. This was probably because I was so active and didn't do a lot of snacking. Since the meals were so good, who needed to snack? My point, though, is that like many of us, I grew up having positive associations with food. Like a good friend, food was and has always been available, interesting, and satisfying. When I conducted my overweight therapy groups, we used to joke that food is better than sex!

I do understand the power of food and the temptation to use it in ways that are not healthy. You see, food became my too-familiar friend after the death of my oldest brother. I packed on thirty extra pounds, not connecting that I was using food to distract myself from the pain of my brother's death. That insight came later.

Not only is food tasty and distracting, but most of us have distorted views of our weight and have fallen under the cultural spell of being dissatisfied with our bodies. I noticed this the other night when my husband and I were watching videos of our children when they were young. After oohing and aahing over the cuteness of our little ones, the first comment out of my mouth was, "You know, I don't look like I needed to lose weight in these videos. I look good. Why did I think I had to lose weight at the time?"

My husband just rolled his eyes with that all-knowing non-verbal communication that develops after thirty years of marriage. I knew what he was thinking: *Linda, how many times have I told you that you don't need to lose weight? And how many times have you ignored me?* We both just laughed.

As long as it is taboo to be at peace with your body, big business will keep making a profit off our "Just five more pounds" mentality. Our obsession creates a billion-dollar business in which the demand for more products, more gimmicks, and more impossibilities is never quenched.

When I look at old photos of Marilyn Monroe, I know North America wasn't always enamored with thinness—Marilyn looks like she could go a few rounds with the ThighMaster! It seems like "thin" got "in" back in the 1960s when ninety-one pound anorexic-looking Twiggy found success as a model. Since then, the fashion and diet industries have been more than happy to jump on the bandwagon and keep the party going (I'm sorry, but it can't be a party without eating!). Consequently, today it appears that the more successful you are, the more you become the incredible shrinking woman.

Take a look at supermodel Kate Moss and recent pictures of Lindsay Lohan, Hilary Duff (Hilary, you looked so natural and healthy when you were Lizzy McGuire! Call me. Let's talk.), and other young adult stars who appear to be dwindling in size as they rise in success. It's scary. They make it tempting for us to think the same way: *that as I dwindle in size, I will rise in success.*

Sisters, it's time to stop obsessing and measuring ourselves by impossible standards that certain fashion gurus decided were *the* look for American women. But we also should not embrace the other end of the spectrum—overweight and obese-—in rebellion of some sick mind who thinks emaciated teens make good models. We need to be healthy, but let's get a grip on who we are and what we believe. Let's get off the scales and get on with our lives!

First things first

Our first order of business in loosening the grip of obsession is to be aware of the diet industry's mission to create an insatiable need for more—and to avoid falling for their antics. Personally, I've had a few victories in this area, but it hasn't been easy. Take last week, for example. I was shopping at my favorite wholesale club one afternoon, walking the aisles with my kids. Near the frozen foods section, an elderly lady was doing one of those demonstrations of a product.

My kids stopped at her small stand and respectfully asked if they could try the "juice" this woman was promoting. "Oh no," she insisted. "Only your mom can taste this because it's a fat-burning juice made only for grownups."

My daughter turned to me with a look of disappointment but also curiosity. "Mom, it's a fat-burning juice only for grownups. The lady seemed upset that I asked for a taste. What's in it? Alcohol?"

You know, it's one thing to mess with adult minds, but leave my kids alone. So I calmly walked over to the elderly lady at the stand. "You just told my daughter this drink was a fat-burning juice. On what basis do you make that claim?" I questioned in disbelief.

She ignored me and repeated her claim to the next customer who walked by the stand. No matter. I can be very persistent.

"You're telling me that if I drink this juice, the fat on my thighs will just melt off?"

"That's right, honey," she said. "It's been proven to melt the fat. If you drink this product, you will lose weight because it'll just burn that fat away."

That's all I needed to hear. I've already written several books on weight loss—all of them discussing the fact that there are no miracle pills, products, or diets for losing and maintaining weight loss. So I stood at her stand and read the product label. In it were the same basic ingredients found in the juice you buy in the grocery store for $2.49.

There was nothing magical about this product except its price of $14.99!

So I did the unthinkable: Instead of falling for the hype hook, line, and sinker, I asked for the proof she was so boldly announcing to our now-growing audience! Of course, she didn't have any. She couldn't tell me which doctors supported the claim or what scientific evidence backed up her statements.

"Why are you telling us there is proof this product works when there isn't?" I asked. "Isn't that lying to all the people who walk by your stand, my daughter included?"

At this point, I took a step back from her demo island. She looked like she was about to hit me. And I think she really could have done it; the look on her face was one of rage. But I stood my ground, albeit a foot away, and waited for her to tell me how she could make such a ridiculous claim. Since she still had no answer, she decided to attack me personally. Following her mean-spirited remarks, she thanked me for ruining her business and her day and asked me to keep walking.

My daughter turned to me and asked, "Why is she telling people that the juice makes you melt fat if it's not true? She's a grandma and shouldn't be telling lies."

"Honey, welcome to the billion dollar brainwash. You're not expected to question the reality of the claims, just go along with them—become a zombie and walk aimlessly through your life feeling bad and searching for the magical pill." And then I added the godly part: "We need to pray that she seeks truth and doesn't hurt anyone!"

I know I'm being tough on the diet industry, but it does a number on all of us. However, the solution isn't for the industry to suddenly become ultra-responsible, although that would certainly help. The real solution is for us to stop buying the nonsense we are being fed and get off the dieting roller coaster. Personally, roller coasters make me dizzy; I can't ride them but once or twice before I long to get off and stand on solid ground—the solid ground of truth. Want to join me?

For those of you who have suffered abuse, grown up with mentally unstable parents, or were verbally degraded, this issue of weight acceptance is more complicated. Still, you can make changes along with the rest of us. Let's quit acting like zombies in one of those old Hollywood horror B movies—walking aimlessly in a trance, repeating our mantra, "Just five more pounds!"—and embrace a different movie image here. Remember *Moonstruck?*

In the movie, Cher's character believes her soon-to-be brother-in-law (Nicolas Cage) isn't dealing with reality. He thinks he's in love with her, even though she is engaged to his brother. In one of the best scenes, she slaps him and says, "Snap out of it!"

Snap out of it!

I like the verbal jolt Cher gives to Nicolas Cage's character. It's a jolt we need to give to each other when we are with other women and talking about how much we dislike our bodies. Maybe slapping each other isn't such a good idea, but let's remind each other to snap out of our weight obsession. Please!

I suggest a gentler version of the slapping scene. I teach this at conferences, retreats, and seminars, and it seems to help break women out of the bad habit of thinking we always need to lose weight. I pass out one rubber band (the kind we use for pulling our hair into ponytails) to each woman to put on her wrist. But wait, this amazing generosity has a purpose. I use the rubber bands to teach an old therapy technique called "thought-stopping." Our goal is to stop the negative or degrading thoughts we make about our weight.

Let's say you wash your hands in the bathroom, look in the mirror, and think, *I'm worthless. Look how fat I am.* This would be an example of a thought you need to stop. When you have that kind of thought, you are to *snap* the rubber band as a physical reminder to *stop* the thought (either yell or think *stop*, depending on where you are and who you're with). The tiny bit of pain felt on your wrist helps you remember to avoid doing this again.

The problem is that we have these negative body thoughts so often, we don't even realize they have become a daily—and sometimes hourly—part of our lives. In order to help us become less like zombies, we have to enlist the help of other women. When another woman hears you express a negative thought about your body, she has permission to *snap* your rubber band and say *stop!*

Let me give you a few examples:

- You think, *I hate my weight.* Snap your rubber band and cue yourself to stop the thought.
- You say out loud during a conversation, "I should lose five pounds." The woman next to you snaps your rubber band and you stop the thought.
- You say to yourself, *Mary is thin, and I'm a fat cow.* Snap and stop the thought.

The next part of the thought-stopping technique is to replace the negative thought with a true, positive one. A lady who has been snapped is to say the positive thought out loud to the women who snapped her wrist or to someone else near her. So the above examples continue like this:

- *I hate my weight.* Snap, stop. "My weight is fine. I'm unhappy about other things."
- "I should lose five pounds." Snap, stop. "Being content is something I value."
- *Mary is thin, and I am a fat cow.* Snap, stop. "Comparing myself to others is never a good idea. I'm not Mary; I'm me, and that is a good thing."

The women are then asked to wear the rubber bands throughout the event, snapping their own wrists when they say or think a negative thought and snapping other women's rubber bands when they hear someone uttering a demeaning phrase about their body.

This exercise can get a little violent, so go easy on your friends and yourself! When women practice this, though, they tell me they never realized how often they put themselves down during

the course of a day. The snapping makes them aware of how frequently negative thoughts and comments come into our brains
and how often we choose to dwell on them.

You can try this simple technique. All you are doing is ending
a bad habit by stopping your negative body thoughts and replac-
ing them with more realistic, accepting thoughts. The point is for
us to move out of the zombie state, be intentional with our
thoughts, and literally, *Snap out of it!* Thanks, Cher!

You might even find a friend or a group of women and work
together on this. I have Jan. Jan gives me hope that it is possible
to walk the mall and not think, *Just five more pounds!* She has not
fallen prey to the media's invasion of the healthy body snatchers,
although I didn't always believe it.

When I first met Jan at church almost fifteen years ago, I was
working in an adult inpatient psychiatric unit treating eating disorders. When you work in this type of setting, you become keenly
aware of the signs and symptoms of someone with anorexia or
bulimia. So, being hypersensitive to the secret world of starving,
binging, and purging, I had my suspicions about her.

First of all, she was thin and didn't appear to have an issue
with her weight. It just wasn't normal! Second, when she and her
husband, Bill, joined our Bible study, where food was always on
hand, I noticed Jan could pack away a good amount of goodies.
(Noticing these things becomes an occupational hazard.) Consequently, it didn't take long before I was convinced she had
bulimia. There was no way she could eat so much and not be
packing on the pounds. I figured she spent her after-Bible study
time in a bathroom vomiting, confessing her secret sin, and vow-
ing not to binge at the next meal.

I was dead wrong. When I finally had the nerve to ask Jan about
her eating (of course, this was done with tremendous Christian
compassion and love), she laughed and explained that her family

is naturally thin and she's never had a weight problem. Feeling like an idiot, I realized Jan was one of those rare women we love to hate—you know, the ones with high metabolisms who can burn off calories faster than we can jump on the scale. But she's also some-body you just can't hate—not only because she's so nice, but because she never mentions weight, and thus never makes me feel bad about mine. And that makes me like her all the more.

We all need a Jan in our lives. They keep us from selfishly obsessing over those five more pounds to lose. So here is my expert recommendation: instead of trying to find the next trend in fad diets, find a Jan and become her girlfriend. There has to be at least one in every town. And it's worth seeking her out. A friend like Jan helps you keep a positive perspective.

Getting off the roller coaster for good

I'm encouraged because, over time, bad habits can be broken, no matter what our past experiences or misconceptions. It doesn't mat-ter whether our negative thoughts originate from the comments of others or from our own distorted perceptions, as long as we know how to correct them.

The complete correction for weight obsession, however, goes beyond stopping negative thoughts. You can think positive thoughts all day long, but if they aren't generated from a true source, they won't correct anything. You see, the positive thoughts we need to know and believe come from knowing and believing God. How He thinks about us is what really matters. His thoughts are right and true and can be trusted because they are never distorted. And true thoughts are healing.

The beauty of when God finds you is that He is very willing to tell you just what He thinks about you. There is no guessing and no pulling teeth to get Him to express His feelings, and no reluctance to do so on His part.

Sounds like the kind of companion any woman would want. Even better, He wrote out His feelings for us in a book.

"Come just as you are," He calls to us.

"Just five more pounds first?" we question.

Snap, stop, and listen.

"Come just as you are," He patiently repeats.

It's hard to comprehend how God could want us "as is"—five more pounds or one-hundred more pounds. It just seems too good to be true. And when something seems too good to be true, we are usually told not to trust it. *Isn't God like everyone else: ready to judge and criticize, or waiting for me to fail? Can I really come just as I am—flawed, confused, and distracted with worry?* Trust me on this: when we're dealing with God, we *can* trust Him. He is that good and that true.

"Yes," He calls. "Come just as you are."

When He called my name, I came, flawed and with just five more pounds to go. There was no judgment, no criticism. Just delight. I am the apple of His eye, the one He cherishes, and my weight is insignificant. He tells me it has no eternal significance. He doesn't place a high premium on my outward appearance but wants my heart. When I finally gave in to the call and took the challenge, the war was over. It can be like that for you too.

And knowing Him speaks to the deeper parts of who I am— to my longing for unconditional love and my yearning for full acceptance. Amazingly, God not only spoke the human body into existence but continues to speak to me today . . . if I just sit still and listen. And when He speaks, the fat on my thighs really does melt away, because He doesn't see it. And for once, neither do I. He takes me just as I am—thighs and all.

CHAPTER 9

You and Me and Body Make Three

Nine-year-old Emily had a loving father, at least until he began to drink. At first, his beer or two was part of a ritual to wind down from a stressful day at work, but by the fourth or fifth one, things would get ugly. "Hey Jell-O thighs," he would call to her. "Go easy on the French fries, or you'll turn into your mother!"

Dad was famous for making negative remarks about Emily's mom's weight. But when he drank, Emily became the direct target. She remembers feeling shamed and embarrassed by her father's teasing. When Dad noticed her saddened face, he blurted out, "Come on, Emily. I'm only teasing." But Emily didn't think it was funny. He said a lot of things he never said when he was sober. She figured drinking brought out his true feelings. Those comments cut deep.

Perhaps you were told as a pre-teen that you had thunder thighs, big feet, or some other stand-out characteristic. This kind of attention usually results in incredible self-consciousness.

When a body part is repeatedly the subject of comment, it can take on a life of its own. A normal-looking thigh can become an obsession. And the negative attention can result in feelings of shame.

When Emily grew, her body shape resembled a pear like her mother's. Her father's comments were still on her mind, and she felt self-conscious for most of her adult life. The crazy part is that you or I could look at Emily and never notice any problem with her thighs. Remember, body dislike is not necessarily based on facts. We bash our bodies because we believe a lie that is usually based on a wound or hurtful experience. Emily was wounded by the comments of her dad. His opinion as she was growing up mattered to her more than the opinions of others. When Emily looked in the mirror, she saw "regular" thighs but thought Dad must know better. He was an adult, after all. So Dad's thoughts became her thoughts. From that point on, her thighs brought her sighs.

Emily's story illustrates the power of other peoples' opinions when it comes to body acceptance. Other people give their opinions whether we want to hear them or not. They judge us and it isn't always fair.

Families are incredibly influential in shaping our feelings about our bodies. When the feedback is positive and there is a healthy attachment with our parents or guardians, we develop a sense of security and esteem. Unconditional love allows a child to believe she can do or be anything. Along with love comes encouragement to take risks and try new things. When we fail or make mistakes, it's OK, because our love is not measured by perfection. This sets the stage for developing a positive self-image.

If, however, you had parents who didn't do much of anything to build up your self-esteem, you may question your worth. And if your parents directly communicated that you were no good, you will most likely develop a negative picture of yourself.

Jill's dad repeatedly called her "lard butt"; Becky's mom used to complain that Becky wasn't pretty enough; Lydia's brothers made fun of her early breast development; Nancy's uncle used to pinch her bottom and make inappropriate sexual comments; Debbie's stepbrother called her "four eyes" all through school; Cindy's crooked teeth were the punch line of many family jokes; and Mary's grandfather used to refer to her legs as "hockey sticks." Unfortunately, the list could go on and on. Many of you could add your own memories to this list.

Even when negative comments are said innocently or in fun, they can create anxiety and insecurity. Being teased for being too small, too tall, feet too big, ears too obvious, glasses too thick, nose too big . . . whatever the specifics, hurts. As a result, you might be reluctant to step out into the world, and you may even find yourself turning down opportunities to grow and develop, which adds to feelings of failure. Self-loathing intensifies.

I've counseled many people who, even as adults, long for parental approval and want to be accepted just as they are. They've never received this. Instead they were pushed to perfection, verbally assaulted, emotionally neglected, or privately shamed, resulting in years of insecurity, low self-esteem, or struggles with addiction and eating disorders. They move from relationship to relationship, trying to recreate the "good" mom or dad they desperately desired. Looking for someone to approve of them, they seek and occasionally find. But what is found is never enough. The need to please and be affirmed runs deep.

Many of us have to deprogram ourselves from negative messages that may not have been intended to hurt us or make us self-conscious, but did. The good news is that we can change the way we see ourselves and move forward in our lives. One important step in this process is to grieve that lost approval instead of searching for it. To do so, you must admit to yourself that you were let down in this area. This can be painful, so tell God about the hurt you feel. Ask Him to take that burden from you. Then give it to Him and don't carry it around any longer.

Next, be realistic about what your parents are able to give you. You may never get the kind of approval you desire from your mom or dad, and you need to accept this as reality. It is a loss, but it doesn't make you a victim. God already approves of you. He esteems you when others do not. As C. S. Lewis reminds us in *Mere Christianity*, "Until you have given up your self to Him, you will not have a real self . . ." Your real self is the one God defines. As your Creator, He approves of your design.

Finally, one of the greatest helps is when people come into our lives as friends, mentors, coaches, teachers, or just special people who can be trusted and provide a basis for the love and kindness we may have missed growing up. We don't have to live as victims; other people will be placed in our paths to affirm us. Do they have the power of parents in terms of influence? No, but as you grieve the loss of what you didn't get, and you mature in your own identity, you fill the emptiness with new relationships that are positive and affirming.

Handle with care

Here's a big reminder to anyone who is in a position to give approval and acceptance: please handle that responsibility with care. You have been given a platform in that person's life—and it's as if you have a microphone and loudspeaker broadcasting your every word to them in surround sound.

As one proverb warns us, the tongue has the power of life and death.[1] It can be used to build up or tear down. My experience with families in therapy is that they often don't realize the power of their words. Sadly, teasing and criticism are commonplace in some families and become the foundation of body image problems that carry over into adulthood. Fathers who tease their teen daughters are unaware of the scars their words leave. Moms who obsess about their own bodies leave a legacy of insecurity for their daughters they never intended.

As we grow and develop, the influence of peers is added to the mix. As teen girls express out loud to each other their dissatisfaction with their bodies, the impact is typically negative. Teens look to each other for acceptance in an effort to feel more comfortable with their changing bodies. The desire to please friends and boyfriends often leads to discussions about losing weight and improving looks, and dissatisfaction can set in during this developmental time.

For example, Jessica was a target of teasing when she began ballet classes. Having reached puberty earlier than most of the girls in her class, one of the girls was very jealous of her dancing skills. Regularly, she told Jessica that she was too big and full-breasted to be a real ballerina. Over and over, she ridiculed Jessica's developing frame until Jessica felt anxious and insecure about her dancing. Eventually, Jessica dropped out of dance convinced she didn't have the body ballet required. This insecurity followed her into other peer relationships as well. When she grew old enough to date, her insecurity was so great that she avoided other people so as not to risk rejection.

Physical characteristics do provide a basis for body image and emotional development during adolescence. That's why it is important for teens to be around others who have healthy ideas about their bodies. In the above example, had Jessica spoken up about the girl who ridiculed her, she might have been helped and the other girl held accountable and directed to stop making the comments. This would have depended on the ballet studio's willingness to confront negative remarks and build a positive atmosphere of encouragement versus competition—something you don't find too often in our society. However, it can be done when peer pressure is positive and pushes those who are being negative to get their mouths in line.

In addition, too many parents are afraid of conflict when it comes to holding teens accountable for their behavior. If we recognize the power of words, we'll do something about the catty remarks we hear. The next time you witness a teen making a smart remark about another person's body, confront her and tell her to stop.

It's not that talking about our bodies is wrong. In fact, it's important that we do this! If we don't, we can't counter the messages or experiences that say our bodies are forbidden, dirty, or shameful. However, we must be aware of the messages we send and receive and make sure they are positive ones. And if we can help our teenagers in this area, all the better.

In the teen years especially, we wonder why we aren't taller, prettier, thinner. Dissatisfaction takes root. We regularly check ourselves in the mirror to look for day-to-day changes and imperfections. When we see pimples, we cringe and feel like they loom larger than life on our faces. Panic causes us to do stupid things like go on crash diets or do one-hundred sit-ups every night. But most of all, we wonder if we are lovable just as we are. Since family support, peers, and friends impact young people, anyone can be a positive voice in the life of a teen. I would encourage you to be that positive voice. The insecurity of this age requires the effort from all of us.

For better or for worse

As adults, we have even more opportunities to be influenced by significant relationships. The partners we choose and the friends we keep and the environments we put ourselves in come to mind. For example, a support group or church small group can offer healing and peace if we let them. A caring, accepting partner is a wonderful antidote to past hurts. Even so, negative body image can linger if it is imbedded with lies still believed from the past.

Those lies can really be reinforced, however, by problematic relationships or toxic environments. For example, a man who cheats on his wife can leave her feeling ugly and insecure. The faithful wife is convinced that the other woman must have been beautiful in order to lure away her husband. In all my years of counseling, this is most often not the case, but that's not what the left-behind woman believes. Beautiful or not beautiful, the rejection that accompanies infidelity produces a blow to esteem and is rooted in issues deeper than appearance.

Women who are in emotionally and physically abusive relationships often find they seek acceptance from the abuser and then blame themselves for not getting it. Date-rape and rape can lead a woman to accuse herself of all kinds of wrongdoing and "fault," and to believe that her body is dirty and shameful. Any type of abuse damages feelings of worth and esteem.

The rejection associated with divorce can play a number on body image, too, especially if you are an older woman. A friend confided that not only was she upset with her ex, but now that she is dating, she feels very insecure about her appearance. "I feel like I'm competing with women half my age for the same men. One of my male friends in his fifties just married a thirty-year-old woman. I can't compete with that. I wonder if any man will find me attractive in my fifties. Dating is awkward after all these years, and I am constantly second-guessing myself. I keep flashing back to all the rejection I felt with my husband."

When alcoholism or addiction is present in a relationship, the sense of powerlessness and unhappiness that comes with it often gets turned inward or is refocused on our bodies, which can lead to feelings of insecurity and inadequacy.

Even when relationships are neutral or positive, most women are vulnerable to the comments of others during life changes such as puberty, pregnancy, and menopause. As the body changes and shifts, negative talk about weight, thickening, and other body transitions can result in women feeling badly about the physical changes instead of celebrating life's seasons and journeys.

The point is that we are all susceptible to the perceptions and comments of others in our adult lives as well as during our growing-up years. Relationship problems and changes can bring out negativity, making us question our bodies and feel dissatisfied. This point was driven home to me when I received the following e-mail:

> I am an unmarried woman with a female roommate. People often misjudge me based on my looks and living arrangement. I am not very pretty. I wear thick glasses that don't lend to contacts. I would like to be married, but so far there is no one interested in me. Would it be wrong to ask God to make me prettier? And how do I handle the unkind comments people make?

You can just feel the hurt in these questions. My heart goes out to her. But asking God to make her prettier isn't the answer. Even though a woman who is pretty does have an initial advantage meeting men, beauty does not guarantee relationship success, high self-esteem, or an interesting personality. Those things must be cultivated over time.

My advice was to focus on the things you can control and work on them. Ask God to help you develop all parts of your being. First, maximize your appearance by taking care of your body so you feel healthy and fit. Wear clothes that are fashionable, make you feel good, and fit well. In addition, update your hairstyle, learn how to use makeup, be fitted for stylish glasses, and walk with confidence.

Second, stop comparing yourself to others and look to God for unconditional acceptance. Third, practice becoming more assertive. When people make hurtful comments, let them know their words hurt. Speak up in a gentle but confident manner. For example, the next time someone insinuates you are gay because you are unmarried and live with another single woman say, "That insinuation hurts." Or, "Please don't judge me. You don't even know me." This may or may not stop the unkindness, but it's worth a try, and you will feel better addressing the issue directly. Then let it go. You can't control what other people do anyway.

Finally, try to do things that involve other people so your chances of meeting men are heightened. Become an interesting person who has a wonderful hobby or is passionate about something. Develop confidence based on other aspects of your life— your intelligence, compassion, kindness, empathy, spirituality, etc.—because that is key to being approached by others. Be positive so people want to be around you. Work on your relationship skills so you become comfortable in social settings and approach others from a position of self-assurance instead of inferiority.

Controlling what you can

Some people handle body dissatisfaction by trying to hide. Others try to control those around them. Neither strategy works. The only control we have is over our reactions to what others say and do. Since we have no control over what others say or do, we have to learn how to love our bodies despite people's insensitivity. So if you are the recipient of unkind body references, focus on *your reactions* to those remarks, not on the person making them.

I remember a time when someone I deeply respected called me a loser. This wasn't a reference to a body part, but the process of hurt and healing is the same, so I'd like to share that with you. It was a mean-spirited remark meant to deeply wound me. I was devastated and began to question myself a lot. This man was getting the best of me and accomplishing exactly what he'd hoped to accomplish—trying to make me feel dependent, powerless, and inadequate. I knew better, though, and had to counter that remark with a lot of prayer and positive self-talk.

Words can't be taken back, but they can be broken in terms of the influence you allow them to have in your life. As I prayed over those words of "cursing," I refused to accept them. I asked God to take them and deal with the person involved, and free me from the grip of those comments. The first step was not to believe what was said. I was not a loser, and deep down I knew it, because I know what God thinks of me. Second, I had to forgive my critic even though he didn't ask for forgiveness and did not apologize for what was said. I made a conscious decision to forgive that person. To be honest, my emotions took awhile to catch up to my will, but eventually I got there.

Finally, I had to release any judgment I held toward this man. For me, this was the hard part because I wanted justice to be served immediately. As I daily scanned my heart, I had to release thoughts of wanting revenge or something terrible to happen to him. Even though it felt unfair that he appeared to have continued success, I had to daily lay that down, knowing God was his judge, not me. This required living out a difficult biblical principle—to love my enemy and let him bring out the best in me, not the worst, and to respond with the energy of prayer. So I did, and eventually I could release this man into God's hands and actually pray a blessing over him—and that's when I knew I was well on my way to healing.

This was one incident. Some of you have had a lifetime of wounding words that have been aimed at your bodies. I would encourage you to examine each word spoken to you that has caused pain. Counter those lies with truth, and forgive and release that person of any judgment so you can move on and live in peace. Don't give power to someone else to define you. They don't deserve it. And don't carry around potential seeds of bitterness by holding on to the offense and hitting your mental rewind button over and over again. It only damages your soul.

When we feel down about our bodies, remember what I asked you to do a few chapters ago. Take a minute and think about the people you admire. Do you have one or two in mind? When you think of these people, do you focus on their body image or physical characteristics? Usually the answer is no. That fact should tell us something. Body image is not as defining as we think it is. In reality, it matters less than the attention we give it. We just have to stay in reality!

If you struggle with medical conditions that influence your body image—cancer, alopecia, lupus, menopause, pregnancy, thyroid, etc.—don't deny the physical changes that accompany the condition . . . but don't allow the reactions of others or the condition or illness to define who you are either. You are more than a condition or illness. If you forget this, make a list of your strengths and remind yourself to focus on the other parts of your life as well.

More than skin deep

To quote a wise old frog, sometimes it's not easy being who we are, no matter what our situation. Kermit the Frog's dilemma was that he was green in a world of non-green critters. But like him, you don't have to let being "green" rule you. As you seek to develop your own community of Muppet friends—those who will love and accept you and support you through the challenges you face—you may find that those people do much to help you see yourself through a new lens, and that is sometimes all the boost you need.

When I was an intern working at a large Veterans Administration hospital, I remember being genuinely moved by the acceptance of those wives whose husbands were wounded and physically altered by war. The physical changes were very challenging in terms of adjustment. What was so amazing was that most of the women were able to look past the missing limbs, nerve-damaged faces, or new wheelchair status conferred upon their spouses and stay committed to the men they married. Glad to have them alive, these women could see beyond the injury and into the soul of those they dearly loved.

Today, most of us can recall the fight former "Superman" Christopher Reeve fought after his equestrian accident in 1995 left him a quadriplegic. For the nine years of his spinal cord paralysis, his wife, Dana, and their three children remained by his side. Reeve's reaction to his debilitating injury was inspiring: "I refuse to allow a disability to determine how I live my life. I don't mean to be reckless, but setting a goal that seems a bit daunting actually is very helpful toward recovery."[2] He couldn't fight discouragement with his physical body, but he could fight it with his mind and emotions.

And of course, there is the incredible and wonderful Joni Eareckson Tada, whose story is familiar to many of us yet whose spirit never tires us. The radiance of that woman's face reminds me of heaven whenever I see her. And when I hear her speak, I feel like a taste of heaven is imparted.

A quadriplegic due to a diving accident in 1967, Joni's life and work is a living testament to the power of overcoming the obstacles of negativity associated with body image and disabilities. Her husband, Ken, married her long after the accident occurred and honors his covenant to this day. He wasn't in denial about her disabilities; he saw a beautiful woman.

Joni would be the first to tell you that the relationship that has sustained her most, the one that has strengthened her—that has given meaning and purpose to her suffering—is her deep walk with God. None of her story is about self-help. It is about the radiance of God seen in her life, shining forth in a world consumed with image but in need of the right focus.

From Joni, we see that beauty is more than skin deep. It has to do with the soul and spirit and our ability to transcend the imperfections of our physical bodies in a relationship that exists beyond the visible. Bound to a wheelchair now, I can easily envision the day of Joni's release as she dances on the streets of heaven. However, freedom has already arrived in her spirit. And that is something that all of us can have—a free spirit, unencumbered by the wounds and hurts of the past, no matter where they've come from.

The power of relationship with God transcends all hurts and wounds. He is the Great Physician, the balm for a weary soul. So be free! Your personal God calls to you. Fix your eyes on Him, not on your flaws or imperfections—and let your spirit soar.

CHAPTER 10

Dates and Mates

It is not easy to become beautiful. It requires hard work, patience, and attention to detail. It also takes a certain firmness of purpose. Beauty is in the eye of the beholder, and it may be necessary from time to time to give a stupid or misinformed beholder a black eye.

—MISS PIGGY

Rhonda dated one guy after another. After two or three dates, the guy usually made some excuse to stop going out. Rhonda was convinced it was because of her physical flaws. Having already had a number of cosmetic surgeries, she was determined to get her physical body "right" so she could attract the man of her dreams. Most recently, she wanted to change her lips.

"You can't even see my lips without lipstick, and even then they're thin," Rhonda said. "I'm thinking about lip implants. The guy I'm dating took me to see a movie starring Angelina Jolie and Brad Pitt. All he could talk about was how gorgeous Angelina was."

"Just curious," I responded, "did he look like Brad Pitt?"

"Well, no, but he was obviously very attracted to Angelina. I've dated this guy longer than any of the others and don't want to lose his interest. I think a few improvements might make me more attractive."

Help me, Rhonda!

"It's OK for him not to look like Brad Pitt but not OK for you not to look like Angelina?" I asked. "Rhonda, get a grip. This isn't about looking like anyone. It's about your anxiety over being single and wanting to be married. As a friend, please look at how phobic you are of men and what you do to turn them off. I've watched you. You come on too strong and then do this weird pull-away thing. It's very confusing, and I don't think men want to work that hard at the beginning of a relationship."

I continued, "Forget the lips, and work on what comes out of them. From what I've seen, you overwhelm most guys on the first date with your intensity. Then you give in too easily on the second. I don't think they respect you by the third. This is harsh, I know. But I'm your friend."

※ ※

Then there is Jackie—already married and disgusted with her body for very different reasons. For years, she has been dissatisfied with her marriage and packing on the pounds, afraid she might have an affair if another man found her attractive.

"I feel so vulnerable to any attention that a man might give me. I certainly don't get it from my husband. He doesn't even notice me. I keep thinking—and tell me this isn't weird—that if I get bigger, he might pay attention and actually notice me when I walk in the room. Sounds sick, doesn't it?"

"It sounds like you can't trust yourself."

"If I lost weight, I know I'd do things I would regret. Part of me wants to lose weight because I don't like what I see in the mirror. Another part of me is afraid that if I do, I won't be able to control myself. I've gone without affection for so long, it wouldn't take much for me to flirt or do something I'd be sorry for. If I want to save my marriage, I can't lose weight even though I would feel better. But the problem is that I hate myself fat like this."

"So the extra weight sort of protects you from yourself? If you lost weight, you think you would fall for another man?"

"I worry that if I was thin and some man paid attention to me, I might have an affair. I wouldn't want to, but I don't know how I would act if a guy really gave me his attention. It's been so long."

"Jackie, you still have a choice whether you are overweight or not."

"I know, but right now I don't trust myself to make a good choice."

❧ ❧

These are two very different women with two very different stories. (Sounds like the beginning of a reality TV series, doesn't it?) However, they share something in common: As much as we hate to admit it, the other half's opinion matters when it comes to appearance. So much so that our body image is based, in part, on men's perceptions. Especially if they're our date, our mate, or a candidate for either position.[1]

You might not like this fact. After all, we are women; hear us roar. But we also want to make sure some guy notices, don't we? Because physical attraction has a lot to do with dates and mates. So what do we do with the realities of that? First, it's important to understand the role of physical attraction in healthy relationships. Physical attraction should exist in order for a couple to have a vibrant and passionate relationship. However, the importance the culture places on physical attraction is way out of balance. It is one piece of the attraction pie, not the entire dessert. But oh, how we love dessert!

Putting physical attraction in its place

As you watch TV or thumb through a magazine, what attracts you to what you see on the screen or page? What do you look for when you want to date someone? Let's face it, physical beauty plays a role for both sexes. In America, we marry someone we love and with whom we have compatibility but also passion. Passion relates to attraction and grows as you come to appreciate the other person for more than just his or her appearance.

Similar backgrounds in terms of class, education, occupation, age, race, politics, and religion also attract. This doesn't mean every dimension of your life must be the same as your partner's— that's called boring . . . or maybe cloning! It does mean that the more similar you are on the big issues of life, the less conflict and stress you will face as a couple.

Occasionally opposites do find each other, but studies show that opposite attraction is usually related to personality, not values. Overall, we tend to look for someone who holds similar values and has qualities we desire—nice looks, similar interests, a sense of humor, empathy, flexibility, good communication skills, self-control, and a good self-image.

What draws people to each other, though, can vary with race and ethnicity. For example, African-American women tend to believe African-American men like larger women. Research supports this belief as true. As a result, African-American women are more likely to accept themselves at heavier weights and feel more attractive than their white counterparts. And the more an African-American woman identifies with her race/ethnic culture, the more "protected she is from the white norm of 'thin is in.'"[2] This is good in terms of body acceptance, but not always so good in terms of health and weight, because a complacency about carrying more weight can place some women in medical danger.

Caucasian women, on the other hand, tend to believe white men prefer skinny women. Well, this is no surprise! White men *are* attracted to thin women (did we really need a study to know this?), and this means white women tend to obsess on their weight and bodies and develop negative body image more so than women of color.[3] However, the more women of color are influenced by the dominant white culture's obsession with thinness, the more at risk they are for body image distortions as well.[4] But the truth about what men believe may surprise you. Read on!

Regardless of culture, one thing men find attractive in women is something called the waist to hip ratio (WHR). Who even notices this stuff? We women sure don't! Basically, this is a measurement of a woman's waist and circumference of her hips converted to a ratio. The waist is supposed to be about 70 percent of the measurement of the hips to be attractive.[5] Apparently this ratio relates to a perception about fertility and youth. As women reach menopause, their waists expand. So evidently the smaller the waist, the more fertile the woman—or something like that.

Now don't put this book down and grab the tape measure to see if you measure up to this .7 ratio! That's exactly what we are trying *not* to do. I'm just telling you this because in one small way it explains the fascination men have with younger women.[6]

Does this mean if we don't get our WHR to .7, we should forget about ever getting a date? Please! No. This just means that when we first meet guys, they have their own ideas about attractiveness. Yet you can still wow a guy with confidence and personality. And look at the other factors in attraction—working closely with someone, having similar likes and dislikes, being together regularly, and having fun. These all play a part in building friendships that can evolve into dating relationships. But we are not being fair to tell people that physical attractiveness should not or will not play a role in attraction. It plays a big role. However, to be fair to ourselves, we need to put physical attraction in its proper place—and also look for dates and mates who can do the same.

We want to be women of substance. We work on developing our personalities, character, spirituality, emotional lives, and family relationships not because this pleases a man (it *is* the millennium!), but because these things make us better people. We feel good about who we are when we are well-rounded individuals.

And keep in mind that this road of attraction goes two ways. Across cultures, women look for male height as the most important aspect of attraction.[7] We typically want men to be a few inches taller than us and perceived as handsome. (Yes, Nicole Kidman is one of the exceptions, dating and mating short men.) And we look for that V-shaped body—large chest, smaller waist, muscles, and erect posture. Men feel the pressure of measuring up as well . . . more of them now struggle with body image acceptance too. Women can be just as shallow as men when it comes to emphasizing physical attractiveness. But we all, male and female alike, need to recognize the role of physical attraction while working on intimacy and commitment.

While there are certainly exceptions to these findings, and other issues involved with body acceptance, these conclusions are generally true. Consequently, how men think and feel about us matters. The important reminder here is to not allow men's ideas to define us; rather, we must understand the role physical attraction plays in a relationship.

The dating game

Will it be Ryan or Charlie? In the two-hour TV season finale of *The Bachelorette*, Trista made the agonizing decision of choosing her lifelong mate. Did she give the final rose to the romantic, firefighting poet Ryan, or did she choose wealthy financial analyst Charlie from LA? Remember, Trista hates the cold, and Ryan lives in Vail. Nevertheless, Trista followed her heart. Romance won over wealth and the mild temperatures of LA.

Quietly, in front of millions of viewers, Trista proclaimed her love for Ryan. Ryan dropped to his knees and gallantly asked her to marry him. Tears flowed. Love was in the air, surrounded by glowing candles and enough flower petals to create a new perfume.

And if you didn't follow Trista's dating escapades, then perhaps you were one of the 35 million viewers who tuned in to the final episode of *Joe Millionaire*, the construction worker who posed as a millionaire in order to see if women wanted him for his money or just him. During the series, Joe wined and dined ladies in the lap of luxury. He had a butler, villa, private jet, cars, and every toy of the rich and famous. When he finally chose his potential mate from a cast of many, she had to decide if love covered a multitude of sins (lying about his wealth, background, and basically his entire life).

Maybe these shows are only entertainment, but they still influence our views about love and romance. Romantic love, as we know it, has three dimensions—commitment, intimacy, and passion.

Commitment involves the willingness to give to another and be faithful to the relationship. Marriage is based on a commitment called covenant, which is a promise made for life.

Intimacy refers to the ability to connect emotionally and in friendship with another. It should be spiritual, emotional, psychological, and physical, and it takes time to develop (more than thirteen weeks of a TV series). It is important for a partner to have the capacity for intimacy.

Passion relates to attraction and sexual response. You should feel attracted to the person you marry. Attraction grows as you come to appreciate your partner for more than just his or her appearance. If you have attraction going and the other parts of the relationship are strong, there should be no trouble with sexual passion when the right moment presents itself.

If you don't feel attractive, ask yourself a few questions:

- Have I become complacent with how I look?
- Do I obsess over my appearance to the point of avoiding men for other reasons?
- Am I overweight and low on confidence?

If you answered yes to any of these questions, your honesty can serve a good purpose. These are all things you can do something about. Taking care of your body, getting to a healthy weight, and losing body obsession will personally make you feel better and also make you more attractive to someone else. And you don't have to wait until all these things are in place to date. I've worked with too many women who won't even try dating until they reach a certain weight. Don't do that! Instead, begin doing the things that make you feel better today in order to build your confidence. Tomorrow will take care of itself!

Mates

At the risk of sounding like we are going the Mars and Venus route here, women do look for different things than men do when it comes to searching for a life partner. Both women and men date people to whom they are physically attracted. In the short run, physical attraction plays a big role for both genders. However, when looking for a mate, women tend to look at resource acquisition—how intelligent and educated men are . . . and how financially able they are to provide. Security is one of our big needs.

Women also tend to look for kindness in a mate.[8] In fact, we want a person who is as kind as possible, a spouse who will be compassionate and monogamous. According to University of Michigan researcher Daniel Kruger, women want a kind, dad-like figure for long-term relationships but a "cad" for short-term excitement.[9] Not always, but generally speaking.

For men, however, one thing we know from studies is that confidence plays a big role in a woman's desirability. Aha!—something we can definitely develop! Men look for that confidence. I remember working with an obese woman who always had dates and could attract men regardless of her large body size. Her obesity was related to a long history of sexual abuse that she was courageously working through.

Despite her history, she didn't let her weight negatively affect her self-confidence, and men found that attractive. She was charming, extremely kind, and smart, and eventually she married a really nice guy. In terms of the women I treated, though, I found her to be the exception. I wish she wasn't, but we are all familiar with the tremendous stigma attached to obesity. Consequently, obese women often lack the confidence to approach a man or go on a date, and men are less likely to ask them out. But a confident woman of any size has a better chance of attracting a mate than a woman with no confidence at all.

Whether we like it or not, though, men pay attention to the female body. They are wired this way. They're visual, and they like seeing a beautiful woman. If you don't consider yourself a beautiful woman (for whatever reason), don't despair. In Shaunti Feldhahn's book *For Women Only*, she talks about an encouraging discovery.

After scientifically surveying men between the ages of twenty-one and seventy-five, she learned a surprising truth about men and physical appearance. The men in her survey reported that it is the *effort* a woman puts into her appearance that matters. Men aren't necessarily looking for a stick-thin woman, but they do care if their wives are out of shape and making no effort to care about their appearance. Men are bothered by women who let their physical appearance go and do nothing to help themselves. In other words, men aren't looking for women to retain their youthful bodies as much as they are looking for women who will take care of their current bodies—to make an effort to be healthy and look nice.

This is great news because it means you don't have to obsess over not having the perfect body. Instead, put your efforts into taking care of the body you have. Lose weight if you need to in order to be healthy and show that you care about yourself. Fix your hair and makeup and try to look your best because you will feel better and your mate will notice your efforts.

So often in marital therapy, husbands secretly admit to me that they are upset because their once-attractive wives have become complacent about their appearance. They are afraid to say anything because they don't want to upset their wives, knowing how touchy any discussion about weight or appearance can be. Yet they are also turned off by a lack of self-care. They want their wives to feel good about their bodies so they can do things together without weight being a stumbling block. According to

Feldhahn's findings, they also want other men to think they did well when it came to choosing a partner. Other men notice if a wife takes care of her appearance. And most husbands want to feel proud of their wives.

If you are getting upset reading this, calm down. Focus on the most important part of Feldhahn's findings: It was the *effort* women made toward keeping up their physical appearance that was most important—not reaching some unrealistic weight or looking like a Ford model. *Effort* is the key word!

Think about that for a minute. Don't you feel better about yourself when you keep up your appearance? When we are sloppy and live in sweats all day, it doesn't exactly boost our self-confidence. And confidence is a big factor in attraction. So it benefits us, our marriages, and our husbands when we make the effort to look our best.

Constructive help

You may be feeling like all this talk about what men like is exhausting. It's enough to keep up with our own issues without focusing on men's issues! But despite what some radical feminists would lead us to believe, there are some good men in America. Some of you may be wondering where they live, if I can provide addresses, and when I will be opening a dating service, but they are out there.

I've been married to a good man for thirty-one years. He does not ever get on me about my body, and he is constantly trying to be that corrective voice, telling me how beautiful I am and how much he loves me. I love that about him. In fact, my husband has positively contributed to me making peace with my thighs! However, I also care about my physical body and make efforts to keep my weight stable, to exercise, and to look my best. Not just to please him, but to feel good about myself as well.

That said, a date or mate can help you feel good about your body when his feedback is positive and encouraging. The issue, then, is helping men see that they can be part of the healing or hindrance when it comes to body acceptance. Since men like lists, here's one you can make that will engage him as healer/helper. Again, though, I want to pull from Feldhahn's research findings. It's important to give this list to your man as a *suggestion*, not a directive. Here are examples of suggestions you can make:

- Tell me you love my body and mean it.
- Compliment me on my new outfit.
- Tell me when my hair looks great.
- Let me know I look "hot" when we go out.
- Look into my eyes and tell me I'm irresistible.
- Tell me you can't believe the mother of your children is such a catch.

I've left spaces here for you to add your own ideas.

_____

_____

_____

These are just a few suggestions. Write down your favorites and hand him the list. Then there can be no excuses for him not to know what to say! Unfortunately, there are men who don't have a clue and say stupid and insensitive things. Those are the men we have to learn to ignore. Of course, I wouldn't recommend ignoring a man to whom you are married. Try counseling instead.

When I do this exercise with marital couples, the wife usually grouses that if she has to tell her husband what to say or outline for him what is helpful, then what's the point? He should just know these things. Well, he doesn't just know these things.

And if he does, he's probably terrified to say anything! The point is that you are teaching him valuable interpersonal skills and giving him ideas about what makes you feel good and builds your esteem. Most husbands appreciate this kind of detail. Usually, they are more than happy to comply.

If you aren't married, negative comments from a man about your body are a red flag, meaning it's time to say *adios* to the relationship. The insensitivity and negativity will only worsen in marriage if they exist before you tie the knot. Don't be one of those naïve women who thinks the power of her love will make the dark side of a man disappear. Remember Darth Vader!

If you are in a marriage in which you feel resentful or bitter over comments about your physical body, you need to address this. Ask yourself:

- Is there some other deep disappointment in my marriage?
- Has the physical dimension of my marriage taken on more importance because there is something else less satisfying that I haven't addressed?
- Am I moving away from intimacy, making the physical part more difficult?
- Does my spouse have unrealistic expectations based on media and other influences?

Ultimately, the encouragement is this: As important as physical attraction is initially in a relationship, it's interesting that no one I've ever counseled lists it as the thing that led to marital success. We should pay attention to this. I've never had couples tell me, "We've made it all these years because my wife has a knockout body," or "Good thing she never let wrinkles cover her forehead, because I would've been long gone!" Perhaps this means we should focus on looking our best, but make physical attractiveness lower on the scale of importance for relationship success.

Cheri is someone who understood this and got it right. When I heard from her, she was terribly upset. Her engagement was off, and the wedding she had been planning for months would be an unrealized dream.

"I don't get it. How could I have been so stupid to think he could love me the way I am? All this time, he hated my body and didn't have the guts to tell me until now."

"What happened to make you call off the wedding?" I asked.

"He said he couldn't marry a woman with small breasts. He said he was having a hard time feeling attracted to me and was worried he might look at other women if he married me. Then he suggested that I get breast implants. Can you believe it?"

Cheri had no interest in getting implants and liked her small breasts. She wanted a man who will love her entire body, small breasts and all. To her credit, she didn't give in to his ridiculous request and knew that this revelation of truth was an indication of deeper problems that wouldn't resolve when she married this guy. She understood that physical attractiveness must be kept in perspective. It's important in every long-term relationship, but it's not the most important thing in terms of sustaining intimacy.

And while the opinions of our partners do matter—we want them to be passionate about us, love us, and feel we are attractive—we don't need to let them define our worth based on their ideal of prescribed beauty. Because when we allow others to do this, we ignore the individuality of our design. And God loves His unique designs!

But God, like dates and mates, desires more. He wants that intimacy and commitment we are willing to give to others. So He established a covenant of love, an unbreakable promise to never leave or forsake us.

Single or married, when we choose God, we belong to a Lover who is wildly passionate about us, sees us as beautiful, and longs for intimacy in our relationship with Him. All He requires is our hearts . . . hearts that will return His affection and be exclusively His.

CHAPTER 11

Victoria's Secrets

My life would be a lot easier without those Victoria's Secret models! First of all, they aren't exactly family-friendly, and they pose (no pun intended) a real problem when we are engrossed in a television movie and the commercials run. Our fifteen-year-old son yells out, "Whoa!" We girls wonder how all those feathers make it through the gentle cycle, and my husband flips the channel as quickly as possible. Hmm. Time for TIVO!

We're not a naïve or prudish family, but those commercials are like watching a short soft-porn video. Gorgeous women sporting mostly their bodies and, oh yes, lingerie parade around for two minutes selling us their incredible sexuality. I like to imagine that this is what my body will look like in heaven. Maybe it's the wings those models wear!

I have to admit, though, that the bodies on these women intimidate me! I don't look like they do barely dressed in those tiny pieces of fabric. Not to mention, I have a hard time paying the prices for such little swatches of material! And who wants to have her husband see the commercials and then see her in the same lingerie? This doesn't seem like a winning marketing strategy to me, but I guess advertisers are counting on men to actually buy the lingerie. Apparently men aren't making the same comparisons we are . . . they have no problem envisioning us in those outfits!

The point is, our sexuality impacts body image. Sexuality involves more than having sex or focusing on specific body parts. It's deeper than looking hot in that see-through negligee from Victoria's Secret. It has to do with how we express ourselves, how we behave in relationships, how we interact with others in general, and how we think about our bodies. Our feelings of sexuality are influenced by our culture (skinny women running around in underwear) as well as our spiritual and emotional lives.

In the previous chapter, we talked about the importance of physical attraction in terms of how others perceive us. But what about the way we feel about ourselves, especially when it comes to feeling sexy?

You know how the Victoria's Secret models strut their stuff on the runways? They ooze confidence when they take those walks. I'm guessing they aren't so confident in real life, but they sure know how to portray confidence at a fashion show. And that's Victoria's real secret. *When a woman feels good about her body, regardless of how others rate it, she feels comfortable in a sexual relationship.*

So if you are worried that your man is evaluating every part of your frame, and you feel insecure in the bedroom, then you are setting yourself up for problems. You need to feel good about your body because confidence positively influences your sexual relationship. In other words, we can be our own worst enemy when it comes to expressing our sexuality in the context of intimate relationships.

when it comes to expressing our sexuality in the context of intimate relationships.

But here is some good news. We don't have to *look* like a Victoria's Secret model in order to enjoy ourselves sexually. We just have to *believe* we look like them—sort of. I mean, we need to have confidence in our sexuality and be able to strut our stuff like they do.

Impossible? Sure seems like it sometimes. Many of us have a difficult time feeling sexy because of all the advertisements and media we view. Thin, beautiful, sexually-charged individuals are everywhere, and as we've discussed, seeing them can do a number on our body image. I mean, how can we feel good about our bodies when all we read is material that sexualizes them?

For example, on the Internet, I just pulled up the covers of three popular women's magazines you would see in the grocery store. Here are the headlines from those covers:

- Give Sexy this Christmas
- Sex Tips from Guys
- Sexy Evening Style and the Makeup to Go with It
- 20 Sexifiers
- Our New Sex Position
- What's Your Sexiest Size?
- 67 Sexy, Simple Beauty Secrets

I don't even *know* what a "sexifier" is! Need I say more?

Of course, advertisers know that sex sells products. Unfortunately, our bodies have become sexual commodities. Physical beauty and sex appeal are the gateways to success and happiness, say the advertisers. We women get the message, that's for sure. But do we want to be caught up in it and actually believe this insanity?

One of the most practical helps I can offer is this very simple advice: Stop ogling these images. You don't want the men in your life lingering on them, so how can it possibly be good for you? In this case, what's good for the gander is good for the goose. The less you see, the better you'll feel. This means possibly changing some of your magazine subscriptions. I'm serious. Stop subscribing, and click the channel when the commercials run. Consider this an act of kindness to yourself.

Church lady secrets

One reason we want attractive bodies is to be sexually desirable. There is nothing wrong with wanting to be sexually desirable, especially to the man we marry. It helps tremendously. I'm just concerned about the path we take to get there.

Let's revisit an earlier comment made by a young pop star. She said she had plastic surgery to "feel good about herself." She's either incredibly naïve, blinded to reality, or not too smart. Does she not see the connection between looking sexy, drawing attention to her music with her body, and selling product? I sound like such a mom when I get upset about this, but I hate the provocative marketing that sexualizes young people. It reduces sex to a primal act and a base pleasure.

Sex by the media's definition lacks the context of love and is separated from intimacy and marriage, which was the original design. In marriage, sexuality can be expressed to the fullest. It is an important part of the intimacy and love a couple shares. Unfortunately, we've lost that connection between intimacy, love, marriage, and sex. However, you can choose not to accept this view and put sex back in its proper context. That's what I'm calling us all to do.

Spiritual women know the secrets of a great sex life. Even though religious women are often depicted as prudes, this could not be farther from the truth. "Church ladies," as former *Saturday Night Live* comedian Dana Carvey used to call us, are a sexually satisfied group of women who, on objective measures of sexual responsiveness, score high! Researchers have been studying this link between religion and sexuality for years. You might be surprised by the results. Then again, if you are a church lady, the data only supports what you probably already know!

Several years ago, University of Chicago researchers released the results of a very comprehensive sex study. Their study confirmed what prior studies reported—that religious women who regularly attend church report higher levels of sexual satisfaction with their married partners than nonreligious women.[1] Here, for your encouragement, are the six secrets of church ladies. Read 'em and celebrate!

1. The lack of sexual experience prior to marriage was found to be beneficial. A church lady who comes to marriage with little sexual baggage is more satisfied with her marital sexual relationship than someone who has been sexually active prior to marriage and may have had multiple partners.

2. The commitment to lifelong marriage and permanence enhances church ladies' sexual freedom and satisfaction. Sexual responsiveness for women depends on a strong and communicative relationship with their spouses. Church ladies are more likely to communicate their sexual needs and be freer with sex because of the covenantal nature of marriage.

3. Common fears associated with sexual promiscuity are absent. Sexual anxiety negatively affects sexual satisfaction for a woman. Church ladies can relax and enjoy more freedom because they typically don't have to worry about AIDS and other serious sexual concerns.

4. Church ladies have less guilt about sexual standards. A University of Connecticut study found church ladies free from guilt about violating their personal sexual standards. Guilt inhibits sexual satisfaction and is found at higher levels among nonreligious college-age women.[2]

5. Church ladies don't see sexual satisfaction as the major factor of marital happiness. Sexual enjoyment is the by-product of a happy and fulfilled marriage, not the cause of it.

6. Church ladies believe God created sex. Sex is not viewed as a physical, technical act to be mastered. It is seen as something godly and spiritual that brings two into the union of one. Sex as God created it is celebrated in the Bible in the Song of Solomon and other passages.

So the next time you hear someone talk about those sexually repressed church ladies, just smile. If comedian Dana Carvey only knew the truth, he'd be shouting, "Now isn't that special?" for a very different reason.

You are as sexy as you think

Robin says she is so self-conscious about her stretch marks that she turns off the light every time her husband comes near her. Laura talks about not wanting to undress in front of her mate anymore. Her protruding stomach embarrasses her. Janeen's cellulite is hidden by layers of flannel nightwear. She can no longer bring herself to approach her husband sexually. Alice won't initiate sex with her husband because she hates her weight and can't believe he would find her sexy.

All four of these women have the same root issue—they lack confidence in their sexual appeal. And yet their husbands love them and find them attractive. Stretch marks, a rounded stomach, and cellulite are part of the package of having children and growing older with a partner. Yet this level of self-conscious pre-occupation will threaten a sex life.

When preoccupation with physical flaws takes over in the bedroom, it can impair our sexual desire, enjoyment, and even the quality of our performance. How we approach this mentally makes all the difference. When we feel positive about our body image, we initiate more, are more active, experiment, and enjoy sex.[3] This makes sense if we just think about it. Engaging in intense self-scrutiny obviously hampers our ability to enjoy sex. It interferes with our ability to concentrate on the moment. And this is tied to body perception, not to reality. So, for example, if we *feel* fat, we don't *feel* sexy. In reality, our weight may not have changed. We might just be wearing tighter jeans that day! Yet the feeling is driving our reality.

When we loathe ourselves or parts of our body, the fallout can be this. We:

- feel we don't deserve to be treated well in a sexual rela-tionship.
- try to use sex to make us feel better about ourselves—more desirable, more attractive.
- act out sexually in order to feel more desirable.
- feel shame and inadequacy, which then interfere with our relationship.
- waste time and energy trying to be someone we're not, rather than focusing on who we are.

One way to handle body image problems related to sexuality is to make a realistic appraisal of your body. Do you need to lose weight or are you obsessing on a few pounds? If you are over-weight, then eating better and exercising will make you feel better. Talk to a dietician or doctor about a good, healthy weight for your

body and set that as a goal to work on over time, not by crash dieting. When we feel good about our weight, we do have more confidence sexually.

Of course, confidence and hygiene go together when it comes
to feeling sexy. There's nothing worse than being in the mood but
worrying about whether he'll scratch himself on that forest growing on your legs! Or worrying that as he is nuzzling up to your
ear, he'll taste the salt from your workout!

Also remember that your spouse wouldn't have married you
in the first place if he wasn't attracted to you. Recall from the
previous chapter that most men won't even date you if they don't
find you physically attractive and sexually desirable. Seeing you
naked is a pleasurable experience for him, not a critique. You fit
his idea of "beautiful," and that hasn't changed. Give yourself a
break and engage in the physical, emotional, and spiritual pleas-
ures of your relationship. Think of yourself as passionate, romantic, and open to your spouse. This will do more to help the
relationship than any cosmetic surgery!

As you might guess, the way we feel about our sexual bodies
is also influenced by our past—by how our parents treated sexuality when we were growing up. If, for example, you were shamed
for walking out of the bathroom naked as a toddler, you may feel
a sense of shame now when you are naked in front of your spouse.
In addition, there is a certain level of identification that plays out
with parents. Say your mother was very obese and you felt this
was unattractive. Any small weight gain may cause you to feel
those same unattractive feelings for yourself. Or if your aunt used
to complain that her beauty was ruined by cellulite, then you may
despise the cellulite on your thighs as well. We tend to form these
ideas from the experiences we have with those we love and
admire while growing up.

As we age, our attitudes toward aging and sexuality impact

our lives as well. If we believe aging makes us unattractive, it will influence our sexual interest. And if we believe losing fertility with the onset of menopause or a hysterectomy makes us less sexually desirable, our sexual desire may wane. However, if we believe the opposite—that menopause and a hysterectomy bring freedom from pain and the worry of pregnancy, we may find this time in our lives liberating. If we don't define ourselves strictly by our reproductive capacities, we do better with sexuality as we age. It's all in our attitudes.[4]

So what can you do if you're in a less-than-great place with your sexual body image? Those negative attitudes may have to be unlearned. Your body was created to enjoy a sexual relationship. You are a sexual person. There is nothing dirty, shameful, or sinful about it when you enjoy sex in the covenant of marriage. Your physical body is a beautiful gift able to bring life and pleasure to you and your spouse in any season of life.

The work for many of us, then, is to reclaim our sexual bodies as good and healthy. The bottom line is that the more you are satisfied with your appearance and don't need others to validate your looks, the more sexually satisfied with a partner you will be. How about that? Something we can actually control—our feelings about ourselves. This means there is hope for all of us!

The secrets of desire

One of the joys of marriage is that sex can be fully embraced in the context for which it was created. But what happens when one partner's level of sexual desire differs from the other's?

Renee described it this way: "It seems like all Chuck thinks about is having sex. I feel like that's the only time he pays attention to me. After a rough day with the kids, I'm not exactly in the mood. But he seems ready to go any day of the week . . . and oblivious to the household chaos. What's wrong with me? At the beginning of our marriage, I couldn't get enough of Chuck. Now, I just want a hot bath and some quiet!"

As a psychotherapist, I've treated numerous couples complaining of low sex drive or lack of passion in their relationships. Frustrated and even ashamed, they are bewildered as to how their once-passionate feelings for each other dwindled to almost nothing. The immediate conclusion is that something is terribly wrong in the relationship. They tend to assume there must be a deep, hidden emotional problem that only Freud could understand. (And if that problem can't be brought to the surface, we can always blame our mothers!)

In some cases, relationship issues are key to unlocking lost passion and renewing sexual interest. Men must understand that women need to feel cared for, esteemed, and emotionally connected to their husbands in order to deepen their sexual lives. Creating an atmosphere of relaxation is important to enjoying good sex as well.

For other couples, an understanding of the biology of desire is needed. Low sexual desire is not always caused by negative body image. In many cases, sexual desire may have more to do with hormones than previously believed. So instead of assuming your relationship is deeply troubled, or that you are creating the sexual problems because you hate your stomach (although this could be an issue), consider whether biochemistry could be playing a role. You may need the help of a physician or sex therapist who can correctly diagnose the problem.

Sustained sexual intimacy may have to be worked on for some couples. All couples face challenges when it comes to covenant endurance. It's important to remember these realities:

- Initial infatuation burns hot and fast and eventually reaches ember stage.

- Sexual desire may be related to biochemical factors.
- Sustaining sexual interest is a complex phenomenon that includes your physical body as well as relationship factors.
- Hating your body interferes with it all.

Dirty little secrets

While it is the desire of most of us to feel good about ourselves sexually, that feeling may be more difficult to come by for some than others. Sadly, we live in a time in which sexual boundaries are regularly broken, sexual appetites are fed by the culture, and sexual violence is encouraged in media.

In this day and age, consider yourself blessed if you've had good sexual experiences in your life. If this is the case, your issues in regard to sexuality and body image will tend to generate more from your own feelings about your body than from distortion and shame that can result from having been sexually violated.

Not everyone is so fortunate. In fact, the number of women who have experienced some form of sexual violation is staggering. It is important to acknowledge this reality by knowing the facts. Sexual violation impacts body image in a way nothing else does.

Those of us who have not experienced sexual violation can't really grasp the full impact these experiences have on body perception. However, sexual violation is real for many of you reading this. And even if this isn't part of your story—and I pray it isn't—you may want to read these sections in order to better understand sexual abuse and how it affects a woman's acceptance of her body. Chances are you know someone who may be helped by this information.

Since body image is affected by sexual experience, and sexual experience affects body image, we need to take a look at what happens when the breaking of sexual boundaries occurs.

Unpleasant sexual experiences can bring on negative body feelings. And if you already feel dissatisfied with your body, sexual assault or abuse can be the nail in the coffin. Typically, a sexually abused woman will avoid sex or act out promiscuously, freeze up during an intimate encounter, feel dirty or shame, and blame herself for the betrayal. These are common reactions to incest, rape, and other nonconsensual sex.

My intent here is to help you understand the body image connection and encourage you to seek professional help in order to work through sexual abuse. Counseling will assist you on the road to healing and recovery. Please know that no matter what you've been through, it is possible to develop a healthy sexuality and fully enjoy married life.

Porn secrets

Michelle has never gone into a topless bar, an X-rated movie store, or an adult toy store. But this young woman has a nasty little habit that is eating her up. Tearfully, she tucks herself in bed each night and says, "Tomorrow night I'm not going near my computer, and I'm throwing away those trashy romance novels I keep buying. I've got to get this under control."

The next day brings hope of a new start. Michelle grabs her coffee, jumps on the train for the commute into the city, and vows to stay clear of temptation. In her huge bag is a steamy novel she picked up at a newsstand. She is bored with the commute and lonely at night. Just a few pages . . . it will calm her down and then she can start her day.

Michelle's journey into the world of porn began innocently with a number of college friends who liked to watch X-rated movies on the nights they didn't have dates. Michelle was drawn to the images, always hating her own body and never feeling sexy. She dated a man who enjoyed pornography as well and who suggested the two of them use videos to enhance their sex life.

The relationship became nothing but one sexual encounter after another, and Michelle eventually broke it off, feeling used and abused. She missed the excitement, however. A friend at the gym suggested she read trashy romance novels as an escape from the boredom of life. Soon though, Michelle found her appetite for more porn growing, and she began logging on every night to chat rooms. The men who engaged her online suggested several links they could enjoy together, and she was hooked.

"I never meant it to go this far. I thought I was just escaping from life for a moment or enjoying fantasy that would break up my dull life. Porn is exciting, and I feel like I'm on drugs when I'm viewing or reading it. Anytime I want companionship, I can jump online and get it. As a single person, it doesn't cost me any money except my Internet connection, so it's really affordable. Lately, I've been wondering if I'll ever like my body again. I feel more dissatisfied than ever looking at images of other women. I want their bodies and feel almost desperate to look like they do. I hate myself."

Michelle is one of a growing number of women who find themselves "addicted" to porn and who feel like it controls their lives. She hides this secret from her girlfriends and family, feeling ashamed and dirty. The pull toward the computer each night feels uncontrollable. And while she knows that her immersion into the adult porn world is creating an obsession with her own body, she feels like she can't stop.

Porn is not just a man's addiction. Women become enslaved as well. And the exposure to chat rooms and erotic images does a number on self-esteem and body satisfaction. If you find yourself addicted like Michelle, contact a counselor who specializes in treating pornography. In addition, you will need to be part of a loving support group that will hold you accountable and help you understand you are not alone in your struggle.

Finally, you'll need to take practical steps like installing strong filters on your Internet service provider and e-mail. Someone else will need to check your computer use regularly for the sake of accountability. Counseling will be necessary to help deal with the images stored in your head and to stop the pornographic thoughts that will race through your mind. You will have to learn healthy models of sexuality and distract yourself from thoughts that take you into body hatred.

The road to recovery is often long and hard, but it can be walked as we surrender the power to God to help us do what we are unable to do alone. Commit to this verse, *I must not pursue the kind of sex that avoids commitment and intimacy, leaving me more lonely than ever,*[5] and make it your mantra. In my experience, body image dissatisfaction worsens with porn addiction because it creates even more reason to loathe yourself. The emotional and spiritual fallout is nothing but destructive to you and others, yet there can still be healing. Begin today. It's a step toward reclaiming your body.

Acquaintance rape

Courtney first met Jerry at a fraternity party. He seemed like a nice guy, and so she agreed to go out with him. A month into dating, Jerry started pressuring her to have sex. Based on her values, Courtney was not interested in a sexual relationship. When she explained her position, Jerry became angry and started to physically overpower her. Courtney was frightened by his response and tried to leave his dorm room. Jerry blocked the door and raped her. She screamed. No one heard. As he pulled himself off her, he said, "That will teach you to tease me." Traumatized, Courtney stumbled out of the dorm. Ashamed, she told no one.

Acquaintance rape is real. It involves a coercive sexual encounter. Date rape or acquaintance rape is probably most talked about on college campuses. It is estimated that 20 percent of college women have been victims of rape or attempted rape.

Psychology professor Mary Koss conducted a survey in which 100 percent of the men who reported forcing sex on a woman said they knew the victim.[6] When you poll college freshmen and sophomore women, you find that many have experienced unwanted attempts at intercourse by men they knew on campus. Sadly, most of the women do not report the attack to campus authorities and end up blaming themselves.[7]

One reason this violent crime continues has to do with cultural norms that condone sexual violence. Male aggression is acceptable. Just check out the latest action flick at the local theater, or watch ESPN for a day. Society also hides behind its assumptions, which furthers the problem. Case in point: We typically think of a rapist as being severely disturbed and, therefore, someone who looks like a criminal or a monster. But research on date rape shows that acquaintance rapists are "normal" men who take in our culture's permissiveness toward violence and act it out on women, often feeling it is their right to demand sex. Violent media and pornographic material support the disturbed view that women are objects to be dominated and abused.

Date rape is an act of violence no matter how you try to spin it. Here's the reality:

- Men who rape use sex as the weapon of attack.
- Rape is not your fault.
- It is not caused by a lack of character judgment.
- No one has the right to violate you.
- You are not responsible for someone else refusing to control his aggression.

- You may feel dirty as a result of the abuse. You may also feel angry at God and the perpetrator. You may even hope the perpetrator suffers as much as you suffer. These feelings are all normal, given the trauma.

Want more facts?

- Nothing justifies sexual violation.
- Women do not provoke rape. We do not give unconscious messages that we want to be sexually dominated by men.
- Violence is not secretly enjoyed.
- We cannot always escape our attacker.

No doubt about it, rape humiliates women and is highly traumatizing. The fallout from rape can include anxiety, depression, sexual difficulties, family tensions, work and social adjustment problems, withdrawal, self-condemnation, apathy, post-traumatic stress disorder, and body image distortions.

Victims often feel ashamed, guilty, worthless, violated, dirty, vulnerable, and fearful. If you or someone you know has been a victim of acquaintance rape, the incident needs to be reported. You are not at fault! You will need help dealing with the aftermath of rape. Contact a therapist or campus authority and get help so you can begin to heal from the trauma.

The key to emotional healing requires letting go of anger, unforgivingness, and guilt. In the natural, this is almost impossible to do. It is important, however, to express your feelings openly in a safe place. God can handle any of your emotions. He created them and knows how you feel anyway. So be honest. In that act of honest expression, you will begin to let go and heal.

Next, work on forgiving the rapist. This is a process that happens with much prayer and surrender. You can begin by making a mental decision to forgive and then work through your emotions as you are able. If you don't forgive, bitterness will fester in your heart and lead to other problems. Forgiveness is something you give even though the rapist doesn't deserve it. It releases you from hanging on to the offense. It does not excuse or minimize what was done to you; it is a gift you give to yourself. Forgiveness frees you from the power of the abuser.

Once you forgive the person who hurt you, you must also release that person from judgment. This doesn't mean you don't judge what he did to be wrong. Rape is wrong. Period. Removing judgment doesn't mean you allow the person to escape being held accountable or that you avoid taking legal action either—it often helps to do both. Instead, removing judgment means you stop thinking of revenge and all the ways you can hurt back. You confront the wrong, take action, and let God and the legal system take it from there. This is an extremely difficult step that usually doesn't come until later in the healing process.

Finally, remind yourself that God does not *will* evil upon you. Renew your commitment to Him. Even though trauma occurred, He will work to bring restoration and growth. Pray that He will restore what was taken. Pray for peace of mind and for the trauma to no longer have power over your life. Find a qualified, licensed counselor who can work you through the process of healing.

Marital rape

"He only attacks me once in awhile. Most of the time he is loving. He does provide for the family, so I figure I can put up with his occasional sexual assaults on me. Besides, I am his wife; maybe he has a right to force sex. My pastor told me to be submissive, so if my husband wants to have sex against my will, I guess I can't stop him."

This is not a quote from a woman who lived in the 1950s. These are the words of a woman living in the year 2006. Marital rape is real, but it's a topic that receives little attention today, despite the fact that it became a legal crime in all fifty states on July 5, 1993.[8] Until the 1970s, the idea that wives did not have the right to refuse sex went legally unchallenged.

There are still plenty of people who believe marital rape isn't even possible. These people often view women as property or objects and feel that married men are entitled to sex no matter what. When battered women have gone to clergy for help, a small number have reported being told to obey their husband—that it was sinful to resist sex under any circumstances. Obviously, this is not the view of most clergy or religious institutions, but it does exist.

It is estimated that between 10-14 percent of married women in the United States are raped by their husbands. This data is usually gathered through interviews with women who will talk about sexual violence. Typically, samples come from battered women's shelters. Thus the numbers may not represent the general population. While seventeen states and the District of Columbia give no exemptions from rape prosecution for husbands, thirty-three states still have exemptions.[9]

Legal definitions vary, but marital rape is generally considered to be unwanted, nonconsensual intercourse or penetration by force or threat of force. Marital rape is usually categorized in these three ways:

- force-only rape, in which a husband uses force to coerce his wife
- battering rape, in which physical violence is also involved before or during a sexual assault
- sadistic/obsessive type rape, in which torture or perverse sexual acts are committed; pornography is often involved[10]

Researchers have discovered that marital rape constitutes 25 percent of all rape cases.[11] It is also not uncommon for other forms of physical abuse to accompany rape. Women who are battered are especially vulnerable.

So who is most likely to be victimized? While marital rape occurs across all categories of age, social class, race and ethnicity, wives under the age of twenty-five are more at risk. In terms of race, African-American women report experiencing rape more often than Caucasians, Latinas, and Asians.[12]

Furthermore, women married to men who view them as property and are domineering are at risk, as well as those who live in violent marriages. When women try to leave their abuser, rape can be a consequence. Women who are pregnant, ill, recovering from surgery, and those recently discharged from the hospital are at higher risk. Finally, those who are separated and divorced are more at risk as well.[13]

The effects of marital rape are serious and can be long-lasting. There may be multiple physical injuries as well as psychological difficulties. Women can become anxious, fearful, depressed, suicidal, and have symptoms of post-traumatic stress disorder. In addition, marital rape can affect a woman's eating, sleep, sense of self, and ability to trust in any relationship.

Obviously, marital rape signals an unhealthy relationship. The misuse of power in the form of sexual violence is wrong. A husband who rapes his wife usually does so multiple times. Because women live with their abusers, emotional consequences are devastating. Rape crisis counselors, as well as advocates for battered women, can provide assistance. The important thing is to seek professional help.

The secret of incest

It happens to babies, little girls, preadolescents, and adolescents. It is confusing and frightening. And it is supposed to remain a secret.

Little Maryann wants to tell someone, but she is afraid. Her father has warned her—no one will believe her, and people will say it's her fault. He tells her that what he is doing is for her own good. So she closes her eyes and tries to imagine she is somewhere far away, safe on a cloud in the sky surrounded by her favorite toys. He's hurting her, so she looks at the wallpaper in her bedroom and tries to concentrate on the pattern. Soon it will be over—at least for tonight.

When Maryann goes to bed, she is terrified of the night. She tucks herself into the sheets as tight as she can and prays her father will not enter her room. But he does on regular occasions. She feels helpless and scared.

I wish I could tell you there are only a few Maryanns in this country, but I would be lying. Incest is a felony crime that betrays the trust within a family. Incest can include inappropriate touching, verbal seduction, abuse, intercourse, sodomy, and direct and implied threats. Here are some sobering facts about incest:[14]

- Perpetrators are men and women, but men commit most acts. Victims are both girls and boys, with girls being the majority.
- Perpetrators can be mothers, fathers, grandparents, uncles, aunts, brothers, sisters, step-relatives, and foster care providers.
- Incest cuts across racial and class lines.
- 66 percent of all prostitutes were sexually abused as children, and of these women, 66 percent of the abuse was committed by fathers, stepfathers, or foster fathers.
- 68 percent of incest occurs in the home.[15]
- Incest is usually repeated and lasts an average of four years.[16]
- Incest may not involve violence but does involve coercion and unequal power. Many children do not report because

they fear the consequences, and thus they live without assistance or help.

Incest dates back to biblical times when sexual relationships between family members were prohibited and punishable by death, childlessness, or community ostracism. In Deuteronomy 27, God cursed the person who committed such an act. When Lot's daughters became impregnated by their drunken father, these acts of incest produced two enemy tribes.

God's ordained order is for families to be undefiled sexually. Yet the perversion of God's plan can be found in church communities even today. Whenever and wherever incest is discovered, it must be stopped and not swept under the carpet.

When a person is a victim of incest, the impact is devastating. There is usually chronic trauma that reveals itself over time. Because incest is taboo and secrecy is involved, children often suffer in silence. But the act and repeated acts affect a child's maturation and development, including body image.

When abuse happens, children develop symptoms of post-traumatic stress disorder. If these symptoms go untreated, they show up in other forms and at other times in a person's life. The most common symptoms include depression, anxiety, self-destructive behaviors, eating disorders, substance abuse, sexual difficulties, feeling detached from your body, physical complaints, explosive anger, and finding relationships in which one becomes a victim of sexual abuse again.[17]

Usually victims blame themselves, believing they are somehow responsible for the horror they experience. Most struggle with low self-esteem and have major difficulties with trust in relationships. Others become perfectionistic in their need to control what feels out of control. Flashbacks and disturbing memories are common, while other victims repress, or "stuff," the abuse.

The power of the abuse by the abuser is enormous. Because

of the mind games associated with incest, it is possible for the abuse to continue long into the teen and even adult years. When a child has been repeatedly told she is bad, responsible for the abuse, dirty, and that no one will ever want or love her—much less believe her—she feels resigned to the way things are. In addition, there are often threats of serious harm if what has happened is ever exposed. The combination of threats and the belief that they are dirty and bad is enough to silence most victims, at least for a time.

Women who experience abuse within their families are more likely to experience poor body image, depression, anxiety, and other related problems than those abused outside the family. This makes sense; children are dependent on their family relationships and unable to escape them without help. This type of betrayal is particularly devastating.

In terms of self-perception, usually a negative identity forms. Shame often leads to feelings of worthlessness and isolation, social and emotional withdrawal, risk-taking and carelessness, self-defeating behavior, and a desire to injure oneself.

Sexually, there is an age-inappropriate awareness, excessive curiosity, compulsive behavior such as masturbation, attempts to engage others in sex play, sexual abuse toward others (especially younger children), avoidance of contact with others, a startle reaction to threats or touch, and confusion about sexual stimulation.

Obviously, these symptoms can signal other family and personal problems, but incest is one possibility. The importance of getting professional help cannot be overstated. The earlier intervention can be made, the better.

Let the secret out

To conclude this section, I want to remind you of a powerful truth. Everything held in secret can be healed when it is brought to the light. Hiding in the dark is where we feel disgusted with our bodies and self. Whatever dirty little secrets you feel you have, let them out with people you trust and who are trained to help you. This is the first and most courageous step on your road to recovery. And never forget: God loves you no matter what your experiences have been. Nothing is beyond His forgiveness or healing. With help, you can be healed and live in freedom.

CHAPTER 12

Not in the Mood

Whenever I visit Boston I make a trip to Filene's Basement, a great bargain store for women's designer clothing. Over the years, I've found that the best thing to do when I go clothes shopping is to wear tights and a leotard under my coat—a trick I learned from watching a seasoned shopper. The woman who taught me would just take whatever she liked off the hanger, take off her coat, and slip the new item on right there in the aisle. If she liked it, the item would be thrown in her cart and she would move on. This was genius. No more being at the mercy of the department store's communal dressing room!

If you've never experienced communal dressing, here's what it's like. Mirrors are placed on all the walls and there you stand, out in the open, no curtains or partitions, barely dressed in the underwear you forgot had a hole in it. You spend the majority of your time in the communal dressing room sizing up yourself and everyone else in the room, and wishing you had pre-soaked that dingy bra! Only you have to pretend like none of this matters because that's what everyone does. It's impossible to concentrate on the clothing because you are too busy worrying about how you look to the other women. It's bad enough having to have to stare at your own body in the multiple mirrors. Add an audience . . . well, it's too much pressure. Once I figured out the tights and leotard routine, though, I could relax a little more.

However, I'm not quite as adept as my mentor. I need the help of a mirror before I purchase anything. So I still have to use the communal dressing room, which means I will have an audience. The other women in the dressing room pretend they aren't looking at me, but I see their beady eyes darting my direction when I'm trying to pour my spandexed body into that swimsuit bottom. The way I look at it is, if I'm going to have an audience, I want some feedback on my selections. So usually I just turn to the group and yell out, "Well, what do you think?"

When the feedback is good, I feel good. However, there are times when people refuse to comment, and the silence makes me think I look awful. *Et tu?* When that happens, it's time for group therapy in the room. I mean, here we all are, baring our bodies in one way or another, pretending like it's no big deal and yet refusing to talk.

I can only imagine the intimacy issues represented among those women who ignore me! If you can't answer a simple question in a roomful of women, you aren't going to do well one-on-one with a man! Ladies, we don't need silence. We need a little encouragement. We need to support one another to make this task easier. We can use the communal dressing rooms of life to bolster each other's self-esteem rather than staring at each other and refusing to speak.

But on those days when my fellow shoppers are acting snooty or refusing to help a sister out by being civil, I am more prone to criticize my body and leave the dressing room in a bad mood. And that's when I'm reminded of something that has been true for me for as long as I can remember: My mood and my body image are related. If we are honest, we can probably all admit there is a stronger connection between these two than we would prefer.

Rachel puts it this way, "If I'm upset about anything, I immediately feel bad about the way I look and begin to criticize my body and think negative things." Sylvia notices that whenever she is in a bad mood, she starts obsessing on her weight. "It does not matter if I've gained weight or not, I just feel fat and can't seem to think of anything else. The more I think about my weight, the more depressed I feel." Tara has noticed that the more upset she becomes with her husband, the more upset she feels about her stomach. "When my husband drives me crazy, I stare in the mirror and poke at my stomach and feel disgusted by the way I look."

It works both ways—focusing on appearance can put us in a bad mood, and being in a bad mood can make us dislike our appearance. On those days when life seems to be going our way, we are a lot more accepting of who we are. Contrast that with days when we are stressed to the max or in a bad mood, and you'll notice that body dissatisfaction grows. In fact, we even estimate our size to be larger than it is on those down days.

How much we like our thighs or any other body part can change daily depending on our mood, because feelings impact perceptions. So we need to pay attention to our mood when it comes to making peace with our thighs.

You can probably guess what gets the most votes for upsetting our mood. If you guessed "gaining weight," you are right. I'm writing this chapter during the holiday season, and I've felt a few extra pounds announcing themselves in a not-so-subtle way. Between Thanksgiving, Christmas, the parties, family get-togethers, going on a cruise (an eating frenzy if ever there was one), and all the confections I received as gifts, my weight has climbed just enough to make my jeans look like they need to be peeled off my body. Everything I put on is tight. So I jumped on the scale to verify what I felt my clothes were telling me.

Though it seems like this would make a person more depressed, it's important to do this when we feel a weight gain creeping up. Studies show that people who weigh themselves regularly do better at maintaining their weight. So don't panic. Get on the scale and assess the gain by consulting the facts, not your feelings. Then do what you must to respond to the truth.

You and I both know how to lose those extra pounds. I'll get back to my normal eating and exercise plan that was severely interrupted for the holidays and be fine. The same is true for you. Just make the decision to do so.

If you've recently indulged way beyond your normal or healthy eating habits, get back to doing what you know to do. With all the billions of books on weight loss, you would think losing weight is brain surgery. It isn't that complicated! Eat less, exercise more. Cut out the trans fat, white flour, and sugar. Don't eat because you feel emotional; instead, eat only when you are hungry, and watch your portion size.

Emotionally, don't become complacent, confused, or convinced that those few extra pounds represent a catastrophe. All three of these things lead to gaining weight. Feeling depressed and obsessing on the gain will only make matters worse. And those negative feelings often lead to even more overeating and weight gain, causing a vicious cycle. (Remember the roller coaster we mentioned earlier?)

Just reengage in a lifestyle of healthy eating and exercise. Both will improve your mood, increasing your success at losing and keeping the weight off and liking your body again.

The triple threat

Overall, women are moodier than men. I know that hardly surprises any of us, but we have reasons for this. Our bodies go through amazing hormonal changes over the course of our lives. Each of those changes represent key moments for maintaining a postive body image. If we don't feel good about our bodies prior to hormonal changes, the changes can worsen our mood and create more body dislike. If, on the other hand, we accept our bodies and embrace the natural course of events, our moods can be managed along with our fluctuating bodies. It's all in our attitude.

Gaining weight is one way to put yourself in a bad mood. Unfortunately, there are others. Menstruation, pregnancy, and menopause are the triple threat to a positive body image. The physical changes can be challenging. It's normal to look at your body and think, *How can these changes be good?* As long as you don't try to avoid or escape what's happening, you'll be fine. The goal is to find ways to celebrate and appreciate our bodies while our hormones rage and our moods swing.

Periodic moodiness

We are women; hear us roar, especially when we are PMSing. I actually threw a phone at someone once when I was premenstrual. (I apologize right now and promise it won't happen again.) Moody, irritable, sad, easily brought to tears—the feelings associated with regular cycling are a roller coaster of emotions. It's a part of our design that I will inquire about in heaven. Meanwhile, here on earth, we've got to deal with it.

Body dissatisfaction rules during the premenstrual phase of our cycles. That extra water weight makes us feel like beached whales for a few days each month. When it finally abates, all is well for the next twenty or so days. Just knowing this should help, but somehow we develop amnesia briefly each month. It's beyond me how something so regular and so ... "life-altering" can sneak up on us, but it happens a lot. However, it doesn't catch the people who love us by surprise. They can usually pinpoint when our periods will begin—and when they have ended!

Changing levels of hormones are responsible for our moodiness. The part we control, though, is how much we allow this moodiness to rule our thoughts and lives. Knowing we won't exactly cherish our painful, bloated bodies during this part of our cycle, we'd be wise to train our thoughts on other realms. This is not the time to stare in the mirror at your stomach or pick up fashion magazines!

Instead, get involved in activities that take the focus off your body and point to something or someone else. And get physical, as regular aerobic exercise helps reduce premenstrual symptoms. If you are really down, pick up a good novel or a funny movie and remind yourself that these negative feelings won't last forever. If you'll just hold on, your mood will improve in the next few days and you'll like yourself again.

Now is the time to be kind to yourself. Draw an aromatherapy bath and soak in it. Practice relaxation exercises like deep breathing, prayer, and meditation. For some of you, antidepressants might help raise the level of serotonin believed to be depleted by the premenstrual cycle. The point is, don't let your mood rule the day, and certainly don't allow it to lower your self-esteem and body image. Remind yourself (and others) that this too shall pass.

Pregnant with mood

I mentioned before that I am sad when I hear women talk about hating their pregnant bodies. This negative take on pregnancy seems to be growing in our culture the more women obsess about having perfect bodies. Pregnancy is seen as an impediment to perfection rather than what it truly is—the glorious experience of bringing a new life into the world.

I know young women who never want to be pregnant for fear they will lose their figures and have stretch marks. Years from now, I suspect they will regret this decision. It's one thing to decide not to have children. It's another to not want to bear them for fear of becoming fat!

Hollywood doesn't help us in this area either. (Are you noticing a persistent theme here?) Pregnant actresses and pop stars are pictured perfectly coifed in expensive maternity clothes, looking like they just stepped out of a salon. Actually, they probably *did* just step out of a salon. Most of us, looking at these images while donning our sweats, don't measure up to what is pictured. And we rarely see these stars with swollen ankles and rounded faces. However, in the privacy of their own homes, these women look just like we do—stretch marks and all.

Women who feel good about themselves and accept the physical challenges of pregnancy will celebrate the changing body. I say this as a woman who was confined to bed for two months, had gestational diabetes, and experienced severe back pain. Still, I loved my pregnant body and wouldn't trade the experience for anything.

Loving your body before pregnancy helps you positively manage the changes soon to come. If you base your body image on the realities of pregnancy rather than how you feel during the experience, accepting the physical changes that are normal for pregnancy is easier.

Not only was I excited about all the body changes, but my husband thought my pregnant body was incredibly sexy. Not everyone is so blessed in this regard. A friend has told me horror stories of her ex-husband's downright hatred of her pregnant body. He refused to sleep in the same bed with her while she was expecting and constantly belittled her growing frame. He verbally and physically abused her as well. For her, pregnancy was a nightmare because of his need for psychiatric help and physical restraint.

Like these two extremes of men, most women seem to either love their pregnant bodies or dislike them. For the first time, many pregnant women experience big breasts and curves that make them feel sexy and strong, and to them, pregnancy is the epitome of feminity. Others focus on the added weight, appearance of stretch marks, and tiredness that zaps their energy. Still others avoid the entire ordeal, feeling it ruins their bodies. And those who struggle with infertility long for the experience no matter what happens to their bodies.

When expecting, body image can change on a daily basis. Some days we love what we see; other days we may feel unhappy and fat. The physical changes cause our breasts to swell, our uteruses to expand, our skin to break out, and our hair to change and even fall out. Cravings develop and our bellies swell like balloons ready to pop. All these new challenges leave some women feeling out of control and at war with their bodies. Even if you embrace these changes with a positive attitude, they take some getting used to. For example, when I was nursing my daughter, my breasts grew to a size F! I felt like Dolly Parton whenever I wore a T-shirt. While some of you may be thinking, *Bring it on!* I became self-conscious and was a bit relieved when the shrinking began after I stopped nursing.

In order to maintain a positive body image during this season of life, it helps to remember that your old body still exists, albeit with these new additions and physical changes. Keep in mind that a pregnant body won't stay this way forever and is preparing for birth by doing what bodies have done for centuries.

Here's another ounce of perspective: Your body is the first world your baby experiences. It is his or her fetal life-support system. Your attitude toward your body is felt by the baby growing inside of you. Cherish this time. What happens is not only about you; these changes represent necessary preparations for your body to develop, birth, and nurture a baby. This shift of focus begins a natural transition to parenthood. Life becomes less about you and now intimately includes another person. Your physical body begins this process of sharing and embracing another life as soon as you are pregnant.

These physical changes, however, do impact us emotionally and influence body image. The mood swings that accompany hormone changes can range from complete joy to anxiety and anger. If you aren't careful, you can begin to loathe your pregnant body by attributing your down mood to physical changes rather than hormonal swings. And if you are someone who is under a lot of stress, body changes can be more difficult to accept. Finding the right clothes to wear, dealing with exhaustion and nausea, and moving with discomfort can add to an already stressful life.

Once you've given birth, another body-image challenge arises. Your body must now adjust and return to non-pregnant status. Many women are surprised that their bodies don't just revert to their pre-pregnancy form. If nobody else is saying it, let me be the one to tell you: the fat cells you developed to nourish the baby in pregnancy don't magically disappear, even if you did not have a weight problem before.

Fat cells shrink with diet and exercise, but they don't go away. I've tried ordering them out of my body, but they just sit there, waiting to be useful again. I've tried to assign them to other people, but they are stubbornly loyal to me! Breast-feeding, which is wonderful for your baby, helps you burn an extra 500-600 calories a day, but even so, the weight doesn't just disappear overnight. Over time, though, breast-feeding does help with weight loss.

New mothers also don't realize the uterus needs time to shrink (usually about six weeks) and won't create a flat stomach immediately after delivery, no matter how many women tell you it does. Your skin loosens and the extra weight stays with you for

Tips for the Expectant Mom

Learning to say no to extra commitments and giving yourself a chance to rest and relax helps. Take time to shop for clothes that make you feel attractive. Check with your doctor and, if you can, exercise. Many women who exercise during pregancy report feeling strong and sexy. Pamper yourself a bit more, too, such as taking naps or getting an occasional massage.

The biggest change you can make to love your pregnant body is a mental one. While you are pregnant,

- celebrate your changing body by educating yourself on the changes taking place so you know what to expect and feel less out of control
- base your body image on the realities of pregnancy, not feelings
- remember, this isn't your "forever" body
- think positive, as your baby feels your attitudes
- relate your physical changes to what they are doing for the baby
- focus on what you like about being pregnant
- remind yourself that your body is sharing and embracing a new life

Focus on your baby and doing everything you can nutritionally and health-wise to help him or her. Ask your spouse, friends, or family members for support. When you feel unattractive and down, ask them to tell you something positive that will help. Thank every man who gives you a compliment. Surround yourself with encouraging people who are excited about your pregnancy. Enjoy this new stage!

a number of months before distributing differently. Hint: Remember, stomachs have rounded muscles—not flat.

I have to admit, I was pretty annoyed with all the women who kept telling me how the fat just melted away after they gave birth, how they lost all their baby weight immediately and got right back into their jeans. I don't know, maybe they were telling the truth, but it didn't help me to hear this. It took me about nine months to lose all the weight and get back into my clothes, and I was eating well and exercising.

Then of course there is my friend Jan, who did lose most of the baby weight immediately. Even though she gained almost fifty pounds a baby, it *did* seem to fall off her body, even though I know that's not possible. With Jan, it's genetics. Love her, but don't use her as the norm.

The sensible thing to do post-pregnancy is to work with your body gradually and kindly. It took nine months to put on the weight—so give yourself at least that amount of time to take it off. Sleep and rest are essential, as the lack of both contributes to irritability and poor moods. Furthermore, the responsibility of caring for another life can lead some new moms to feel over-whelmed and may overintensify their dislike of their bodies.

Commit to healthy eating, not dieting, especially if you are nursing. Reduce portions and don't skip meals. Drink water. Stay fit and exercise with your baby. Be realistic about your goals and consider the additional responsibilities you now have that require more of your time. Be patient and don't compare your body to the stories of others. You and your experience are unique.

Mental pause

My entire married life, I have been the cold one. Living in the Chicago suburbs, I used to pile on the covers at night, wear those woolen footies, and practically sleep in my robe. Well, sleeping with me these days is a different story—my husband isn't certain he's with the same woman! I now have shorts and tank tops for pj's, and it takes only seconds in bed before I throw off the cov-ers and let every body part become as exposed as possible. I jump up to turn on the fan and wonder if we should consider Canada for retirement. Either we are experiencing global warming or something is going on with me. I suspect it's the latter.

Menopause is the final body transition caused by hormone changes. I am convinced that our attitude going into menopause has everything to do with how well we manage it. Most of us need a new perspective on what it means to get older, considering the overemphasis on youth and beauty in our culture. Here's your first perk: Think of menopause as a time when you can save on bedding and sleepwear!

I will discuss aging and body acceptance in the next chapter, but for now, at least know this: If our attitude toward menopause is negative, we can change it. Viewing a hot flash as a power surge certainly helps lighten our mood. And most of us need a lot of lightening up during this life transition. We get a little touchy. Maybe a bit irritable. OK, some of us get downright depressed thanks to the hormonal changes.

Think of menopause as a destination, a place we all end up, so why not make the journey as enjoyable as possible. In terms of time, menopause is the year after your last period stops. Perimenopause is the transition leading up to that point. It is during the perimenopause state that most women experience hot flashes, night sweats, irritability, mood swings, insomnia, and other symptoms. The transition to menopause can take years, even decades, as our hormones try to balance and finally stabilize. And like puberty, the transition does finally complete, thank God!

If you have a personal history or family history of depression, you are more likely to experience depression during menopause. With that depression comes feelings of self-loathing or poor body image. So be aware of your history and seek professional help. Overall, the more negative our attitudes about body changes and the more we approach this phase of life with dread or agitation, the more difficulty we will have with body image and acceptance. Thus, we need to take a mental pause and reevaluate our attitudes toward menopause.

If we think of this hormonal change in purely physical terms, there is one tremendous reward: menstruation stops. Grieving our ability to reproduce is normal, but so is celebrating the freedom from menstruation. When I packed the last tampons and pads away for my daughter, I wanted to party. After all those years—freedom! It was truly exhilarating!

And the physical benefits don't stop there. The monthly cravings and binges associated with our periods usually end. We have regular cycles of energy and feel less fatigued when we finally get through the changes. Breast tenderness ceases. And yes, our moods even out, no longer tied to the up-and-down hormonal cycle of our periods.

We are often told that our sexual drive lowers significantly during menopause, but a new study says no. Blaming our lowered sex drive on hormones may be a mistake. It appears that lowered sexual desire may actually be caused by negative body image! That's right—negative body image, not hormones.[1] In fact, middle-aged women who feel positive about aging also feel an enhanced sense of desirability and sexuality. As I stressed in chapter 11, attitude matters when it comes to body image! Aren't you relieved to know I'm not just making this up?

In our age-obsessed society, it behooves us to concentrate on the pros and not the cons of menopause in order to keep our mood steady and deal realistically with the changes. Emotionally, spiritually, and psychologically, menopause brings change that can be celebrated. This is usually a time of self-knowledge and self-confidence. Spiritually, we mature and can deepen our walk with God if we concentrate on this part of who we are.

If emotional issues from your childhood resurface at this point in your life, get therapy and work through them. Forgive those you need to forgive. Don't hold grudges or stay angry at people who have hurt you. Take control of your reactions by choosing to be a grown-up in all areas of your life. Maturity is a time to not only make peace with your thighs, but with other people too.

During this life stage, more time is usually available to concentrate on what you like to do or have always wanted to do. New hobbies and skills can be developed. Hire a life coach and embark on a path you've been thinking about for years but have been afraid to explore. Write in a journal and express your feelings and thoughts. Take time to pamper yourself a bit. Make that spa appointment—and don't feel guilty! In other words, don't listen to the cultural stereotypes that portray menopause as some sort of disease to be endured or the end of your desirability as a woman. *Carpe diem!*

From puberty to pregnancy to menopause, we can celebrate and embrace our changing bodies if we only decide to do so. If you appreciate the female form and all the wonders of change that accompany it, your mood will be lifted. Choosing acceptance will impact your ability to make peace with your thighs and feel joy, no matter what happens physically.

In the mood

Since mood very much influences body image, and body image influences mood, we need to stay positive and keep moving forward in life. I want to suggest three additional areas that will help—placing yourself around positive people who will compliment you, becoming more assertive and confident in the way you deal with people and life, and incorporating *moderate* exercise into your life. All three of these things are easy to do, inexpensive, and will boost your mood and your body image.

Words have weight

Because so many of us struggle with negative body image and have done so for years, it is amazing to me that one method of help involves something so easy. Simply stringing together a few words of affirmation is healing for our souls. Compliments make us feel better about our bodies and who we are. New research shows that giving a woman a compliment about her character or appearance is enough to make her feel better about herself. It doesn't seem to matter which type of compliment is given, but that it *is* given. And the compliment can be relatively mild: "You sound like a nice person" will do the trick.[2]

Compliments are easy to hand out, but we need people in our lives who will give them to us. We all like to be praised. From the time we are little girls and want Daddy to tell us how proud he is of our bike riding, our beautiful smile, or our kind heart, we never outgrow the need for affirmation. If you live with people who do nothing but criticize and tear you down, find friends who will genuinely compliment you. Develop a network of positive people. And for those times when your "praise team" isn't around, keep a Warm Fuzzies file on hand with the affirming notes, cards, and e-mails you've received from others so you can reference them on a down day.

Many of us have to learn to accept compliments, too, don't we? I had such a difficult time with this when I was first married. My body image was at an all-time low. My poor husband would tell me how beautiful I was and I wouldn't believe him. He would compliment me and I would minimize it and secretly think he was just making things up because we were married. Crazy, huh?

Anyway, he became so frustrated with me that he made me pratice responding to his compliments positively. I could only say "thank you," and smile. After enough practice, I became good at receiving. But inside I knew the difficulty I was having related not only to believing him, but believing anyone. My low self-esteem and feelings of inadequacy were the true culprits that had to be confronted.

As I mentioned before, the place where I found healing was through an authentic relationship with God. His unconditional love and grace, His delight in me, His unchangeable nature—all were what I needed to experience in order to know I was worth loving and complimenting. In addition, having people around me who valued me and were able to express this helped tremendously.

True love brings adoration and gushes of praise. It flows from the very fabric of who we are and lavishes the loved one with every good thing possible. When we've experienced that kind of love, it isn't so difficult to give it to others or to receive affirmation of our worth.

Speak up

"Sure, I'll cook for the spaghetti dinner." "Yes, I can babysit your children for the day." "I suppose I can chair another committee." "Since no one else will volunteer, I guess I'll do it." Do you ever find yourself saying these things, only to realize in a quieter moment that you've taken on too much and committed to doing more than you can realistically handle? Then you get stressed and start kicking yourself for not saying no.

We often take on too much because we don't know how to say no. Maybe we are afraid to speak up or don't feel we have the right. Sometimes our inability to be assertive is because we feel a need to please others or want to be loved for what we do. Other times we might feel we have to be Superwoman and do it all.

Well, it's time to turn in your cape! To learn to say no and not feel guilty. You'll not only reduce the stress in your life and improve your mood, but also improve your body image. That's right . . . women who see themselves as strong and assertive have fewer problems with body image than those who are passive. Assertiveness has to do with being able to ask for what you want or need. When you are able to do this, it builds confidence and self-esteem. Both are related to a positive body image.

Assertiveness is behavior that falls somewhere between giving in and aggressiveness. It is not resentfully surrendering to the wants of others or keeping silent and expecting people to read your mind. It is also not yelling at people and demanding your way. It is a practiced skill that helps you set limits and talk about your needs without feeling guilty. Contrary to popular belief, you don't have to be angry to be assertive. In fact, staying calm is preferred.

There are two parts to being assertive. First, you have to know what you want. Second, you have to say it. One reason so many of us aren't assertive is because we don't know what we want. When we don't have a clue about our desires or needs, we leave ourselves open to the manipulation or expectations of others. We're much more likely to allow someone else to talk us into doing things and then feel resentful later because we have too much on our plate. Or we feel guilty and believe we don't have the right to protect our time.

Don't stay in that place. Speak up and let your voice be heard. It's one way to improve your mood. When you address problems as they occur, you won't build up anger and hold on to feelings and thoughts that can grow into bitterness. Oftentimes, passivity and helplessness are roots of depression, anxiety, and other negative emotions that impact our mood.

If you've never learned this skill and are unsure how to be assertive, read on. Here is a step-by-step description so you can work on it:

1. *Evaluate the situation.* Do you really want to do what is being asked—or does it feel like an obligation? Do you like the way things are going? Are you feeling bothered? If you don't act, will you feel resentful, upset, anxious. or down?

2. *Decide when to be assertive.* Should you speak up immediately, or do you need time to think about how you feel and what the consequences of addressing the situation might be? Perhaps you want to organize your thoughts, or decide if you are reacting to the issue at hand, or take time to build up some courage. Knowing when to confront is important. For example, asserting yourself when your spouse is drifting off to sleep, or confronting an alcoholic when he or she is drunk, is a waste of time. Time your confrontation for a moment that is conducive to listening and responsiveness.

3. *Identify the problem.* Be specific. Don't expect others to read your mind or magically guess your distress or need. Say exactly what the problem is and how it is affecting you.

4. *Say how you feel.* No one causes you to feel things. You allow yourself to feel things. Don't blame others. For example, instead of saying, "You make me mad when you come home late," say "I get upset when you come home late." Your purpose is to communicate the feeling that is associated with something negative from your point of view.

5. *Say what you want to have happen.* This is the tough but important part. You need to know what you want and what would help the situation. For example, "I would like you to call me if you are going to be late. Try to make it home by 7:00 P.M. each evening." It is vital to communicate a solution or desire so that the other person has an idea about how to remedy the problem. This doesn't guarantee the person will do what you request, but at least you've communicated what would help and can negotiate from there.

When we learn to assert ourselves, we take charge of our feelings and validate the needs we have rather than internalizing anger or feeling that we aren't worth anything. Being passive or swallowing our feelings leads us to glare more often at the image we see in the mirror . . . or to drown our troubles in a bowl of chocolate. But taking care of our internal emotional lives prevents us from beating up on our physical appearance.

Assertiveness is a skill you can practice and benefit from doing. Rather than focusing on the size of your lips, use them to feel more confident and in control by speaking your mind.

Get moving

Harvard Medical School's Dr. Ratey says, "It is helpful to think of the brain as a muscle. One of the best ways to maximize the brain is through exercise, [through] movement. Everybody feels better after exercise. There is a reason for it."[3] When we exercise, there are biochemical changes in the brain that work to our advantage. For example, during exercise we generally don't worry. When there is no worry, brain cells get renewed because the worry cells are resting.[4] So, if you don't worry when you exercise, you are helping your brain and your body. Also, endorphins, which are neurotransmitters in the brain, are increased and released during exercise. Endorphins naturally relieve pain, which helps us feel good.[5]

When you exercise, it helps to follow these guidelines in order to improve your mood and body image. The exercise should be 20-30 minutes long; of moderate intensity; happen regularly; involve rhythmic breathing; have predictable and repetitive movements; and not be seen as competitive with the people involved.[6]

While we all need to exercise for health and mood reasons, we have to guard against doing it excessively. While researching for an article on midlife eating disorders, I came across a group of women called "Anorexercisers." These are women who calculate every calorie they eat and feel compelled to burn them off through rigorous exercise. They exercise compulsively. It's their way of attaining power and control over their lives. Eventually, exercise begins to control them and leads to these women suffering insomnia, depression, and fatigue, in addition to physical injury and dehydration.

When exercise interferes with your daily activity or becomes the focus of your thoughts, you've probably crossed a line and need to limit your time in the gym or wherever you work out. It's too easy for this activity to become just another way of avoiding other problems in our lives, like a drug used to numb out the dissatisfaction or inadequacy we feel. Instead of being an outlet for stress and a way to improve mood and body image, exercise becomes a coping mechanism and addiction. The goal is to do moderate exercise for health reasons, not to use exercise to obsess on your body even further.

Compulsive exercise will never be a problem for me. If you are one of those perky people who love it, e-mail me and tell me your secret, because I just can't get there. Once upon a time, I ran two miles every day, six days a week, for two years. And you know what? I couldn't stand it. I never once got that runner's high—not even a little!

If the truth be known, I hate to exercise. Well, hate might be too strong. At the very least, though, I don't enjoy taking the time to do it. The entire time I'm on the treadmill, I'm thinking about what else I could be doing and enjoying right then if I weren't exercising. I do everything I can to make the time pass.

I've tried reading—not possible with all the bouncing; television—can't hear it due to the motor on the machine; lifting weights—usually I lose my balance and fall off. The only less boring thing I can think of is to become a college cheerleader again. I know that sounds nuts, but if I run with my feet and do the cheers with my arms, the time passes faster. I'm ready if the University of Michigan ever calls me to fill in for someone.

After I've exhausted all the cheers I can remember, I use the time to meditate. With my headphones on and iPod handy, I tune in to uplifting music and think about the lyrics. I look out at the marsh behind my house and appreciate the beauty around me. It's a time to be quiet and consider the many blessings I have. It's also a time to pray. My mind and body are engaged and my spirit is lifted. So even though exercise is boring to me, I keep subjecting myself to it because it's beneficial.

I notice a distinct improvement in my mood and feelings about myself when I regularly "get physical." Paying attention to this and reminding myself that this good feeling will return if I keep it up is at least a slight motivation. Sometimes we just have to be the grown-up and do the boring but beneficial thing!

Perhaps one of the reasons so few of us exercise regularly is because it requires taking time out for ourselves—something we women have difficulty doing. Personally, I've decided to commit to that time and consider it to be like depositing into my own savings account. I have to take care of me in order to be any good to others.

We often have trouble staying consistent and doing things for the long-term benefits. That's when friends help again. When I have difficulty getting motivated to exercise, I ask a friend to do it with me. Usually one of us can get the other one going. I'd still like to find another ex-college cheerleader and learn more cheers. This would eat up more time on the treadmill. If you are interested, you have to be from the Big Ten or ACC to qualify! In all seriousness, do find a reliable friend who will commit to walking with you every morning or evening, or will meet you at a club, or ride bikes, or do something you can sustain on a regular basis.

Please give exercise a try. It can be a daily walk, a run through the park, pushing the stroller through the neighborhood, rollerblading down the street, a game of tennis or racquetball, or swimming laps. Try different activities until you find something that works and can be done regularly. It's one more thing in our arsenal of weapons that helps fight negative body image. And if you know something works, it's a good idea to do it whether you love it or not. After all, you're worth it.

CHAPTER 13

Youthanasia

Why hope to live a long life if we're only going to fill it with self-absorption, body maintenance, and image repair? When we die, do we want people to exclaim "She looked ten years younger," or do we want them to say "She lived a great life"?

—ANONYMOUS

"Bat-wing deformity." That's the term plastic surgeons use to describe the extra skin that hangs from the upper arms when a person ages. Nice, huh? "Aging neck deformity" is wrinkled neck skin.

To hear that kind of talk, you'd think aging is a disease. It's not, but we are getting dangerously close to treating it as such, given our cultural obsession with turning back the clock and discovering the fountain of youth. With all the ad talk about "younger looking skin, "a skin you love to touch," "having a schoolgirl complexion," and then the ultimate, "Don't lie about your age, defy it," why wouldn't women feel pressed to look younger? But what the advertisers never mention is that if we buy into thinking we have to shave years off our appearance in order to be happy or successful, our body image suffers.

I'm not suggesting that resisting the cultural pressure to look young is easy. When I was outlining this book, I debated whether or not to talk about my age. I didn't debate long. How could I write a book on body image and not deal with my own aging process? But I am not so enamored with it that I go around announcing my age all the time or greet strangers with, "Hi, I'm Linda. Do you know how old I really am?"

If age does come up in a conversation, I'm at the point now where I'm starting to think, *Why should I hide it or, worse yet, lie or defy it?* I thought the truth was supposed to set us free! Honestly, though, when it comes to aging, I'm still in process, trying to lose my hang-ups, understand my conflicting feelings, and resist cultural prescriptions. I'm no different than you are when it comes to wanting to look good but having to decide where to draw the line.

One thing I do know: to deny my age isn't the answer. That said, the reality is that we'd all like to defy the physical aspects of aging to some degree. Recently I've been challenged to neither deny nor defy. Let me explain.

The gauntlet was thrown when I turned fifty. I confess, I didn't like it. I mostly didn't like the sound of it. It was much easier to tell people I was forty-something. When I awakened on my fiftieth birthday, I prayed no one but my mom and dad would remember this special day. (To them, I'm still a youngster.) With trepidation, I tiptoed to my living room window, hoping my neighbors hadn't planted lighted plastic crows and pink flamingos in my yard with a sign saying, "Linda is fifty. Isn't it nifty?" Thankfully, they spared me. Others in our cul-de-sac have not been so fortunate.

On that day my husband, Norm, was very kind to me. He sensed I wasn't in a celebratory mood. We simply went out for dinner, just the two of us. Later we celebrated with a few other couples, some of whom had already reached the half-century mark.

During our intimate dinner, Norm and I marveled at how long we had been married, but also how we still felt like young college kids ready to take on life . . . only our bodies didn't quite feel the same. I'm pretty sure I wouldn't be able to be thrown off a cheerleading pyramid and land on my feet at this stage of life. I would only land in a hospital! But one of the fun things about being married young is that you can just look at each other and be twenty-four years old again in your mind and memories.

Thankfully, Norm allowed me to ease into the new decade by not making it a big deal and saying all the right things. And at the end of the day, I realized the decade shift wasn't so bad. I didn't feel any different. I couldn't see any major changes in the mirror, and I was doing my best to be healthy and fit. I had a great husband, two wonderful children, and a fulfilled life—my blessings were many. I also no longer struggled like I used to with the uncertainty of who I am or what my purpose is in life. And I now had an inner contentment I didn't experience when I was younger.

Come to think of it, turning fifty felt like I was finally a full-fledged grown-up. Now I am getting notices from the AARP and reading books about aging gracefully. (I know, this probably should have happened sooner.) In just a few years I'll be carded again, only this time it won't be to determine my movie eligibility but to get those movie discounts! Along the way, I'm learning that age is relative. (I just wish it was my relative that turned fifty and not me!)

As the days passed, I was adjusting well to my new decade. Until the local newspaper ran a story about my latest book, *Overweight Kids*. The article began, "Dr. Linda Mintle, 50, has written . . ." I don't even remember what they said about the book, just that they mentioned my age in the first line of the article. Was that really necessary? Please explain to me what being fifty has to do with writing a book about preventing overweight kids. I wanted to wring the neck of the interviewer, as any menopausal woman would! Fortunately for that person, I resisted my violent impulses (an ability that improves with age!) and forced myself to accept the fact that now the entire community knows how old I am. Bring on the crows and flamingoes!

I think one of my problems with adjusting to this age is that I was always the youngest. I was the youngest in my family growing up. I was the youngest in my class all through school. I started college at seventeen and was married just shy of twenty. I moved up quickly in my career and held positions usually reserved for older, more seasoned clinicians. Even my husband is a few years older. So to make me the oldest in any group is just not right!

But I couldn't escape the facts when I became a mom. Looking back at my years of infertility, I suspect this was God's way of preparing me for turning fifty. I tried to become a mother at a younger age, but it didn't happen until I was thirty-five and then thirty-eight. I know this isn't a big deal today, but at the time, having babies at that age made me a dinosaur.

I'll never forget the year I attended my daughter's class tea for her kindergarten class. We had just moved to the Chicago area, so my kids were enrolled in a new school. As I sat in the circle of women at the tea talking about loose teeth (not mine, our children's), someone had the bright idea that we should introduce ourselves and say how long we'd been married. The ladies thought this was brilliant. I wasn't so sure.

A few ladies volunteered to begin, proudly announcing that they'd been married six, eight, even ten years. People clapped and marveled at the accomplishment. Then it was the turn of the woman sitting next to me. She appeared just a little too perky for my liking. When she introduced herself, she mentioned the year she graduated from high school. *High school?* I'd been out of *graduate* school and working in my career for the past ten years! I couldn't even remember high school! This wasn't a good sign.

Suddenly I panicked, thinking, *Could she be* my *daughter? Could I be old enough to be her mother?* I quickly did the math. With a sigh of relief, I realized it was close but not possible. Meanwhile, she continued to talk and giggle a lot, although I don't think anyone told a joke. Finally, when she informed us that she had been married for just over five years, I got it: her kindergartner was a honeymoon baby. From that point on, the babies kept coming, she said. She was now pregnant with number four.

At that moment I realized it was my turn. I needed to stop staring at her. People were waiting for me to speak. With "four babies in five years" and *But she looks like she's still in high school* battling it out in my head, I was at a loss as to what to say next. Was I really going to tell these women I had been married twenty-four years after Shirley Temple's double had just spoken? Looking at all those cellulite-free legs in the room, I decided against it and instead made a joke. "I've been married forever. It's amazing I'm even alive to tell you about it. Next."

As you can tell, it took me a few weeks (OK, months) to come to grips with the fact that fifty didn't mean Game Over. I want to thank all my relatives for still referring to me as young. It helped during the transition until I was able to realign my thinking and kick myself in my sagging rear.

But seriously, middle age is a good thing and needs to be celebrated more in our culture. If you don't believe it, go out and buy a copy of Dale Hanson Bourke's book *Second Calling*. She and her friends will confirm what I'm experiencing—the later seasons of life are a time of tremendous productivity and achievement. They bring a new serenity that comes from knowing who you are and finally liking that person, if only we will come to accept aging as inevitable. Sadly, we usually work against ourselves here. We let our own crazy thoughts, reinforced by the larger culture, keep us from peace and the positiveness of quiet acceptance.

So what's a woman to do? The first step is to know what you're fighting.

Fight against youthanasia

Youthanasia is my word. I made it up, so let me define it for you. Related to its cousin, *euthanasia*, the word *youthanasia* is a noun meaning the act or practice of killing an individual's spirit in a relatively painless way that appears merciful—at least to people who are under forty.

When you are *youthanized* (the verb form), you are slowly devalued by others for getting old, and that devaluation grows on you until you feel irrelevant and worthless. All-out attempts to eliminate aging are made, with fear being the primary motivator. Looking young and beautiful at all costs is the goal. If you don't hit the mark, you are youthanized by a culture unsympathetic to aging. No one comes right out and tells you this—that would be too cruel. Instead, you are quietly dismissed as over the hill and put out to pasture, all the while being led to believe that healthy aging doesn't exist.

Even though you didn't get to vote on the use of youthanasia, it is widely practiced every day in American culture, particularly by the media. We aging women are told that unless we are young and beautiful, we won't be happy, successful, healthy, or relevant. As pop artist Annie Lennox declared decades ago, "Keep young and beautiful. It's your duty to be beautiful. Keep young and beautiful if you want to be loved." And boy, do we try!

We are all too aware that older faces are not exactly popular in films, fashion, television, or advertisements unless the subject relates to aging or disease. So in order to avoid youthanasia, we fall for all the traps—laser hair removal, Botox injections, permanent makeup, dermabrasion, cosmetic surgeries. Staying youthful is like constantly updating our wardrobes. There is a room full of new things to try on for the sake of looking better— we just have to purchase the products and procedures.

Forget the risks of tampering too much with the human body. Our goal is to stay young and beautiful if we want to be loved. Clinical psychologist Stanley Teitelbaum sums it up well: "In the eyes of society, when you're 20 you're hot; when you're 40, you're not; and when you're 60, you're shot."[1] Can't you just hear *Fiddler on the Roof*'s Zero Mostel singing, "Youthanasia!"?

"The good news is that even as we get older, guys still look at our boobs. The bad news is, they have to squat down first."

Even looking beautiful doesn't guarantee a good body image as you get older. In fact, women who are used to getting attention for their looks have a harder time with aging than us regular-looking folks.[2] A woman has been fully youthanized when she has allowed society to put to death the hope of embracing and— dare I say it?—thriving within the natural aging process. And it usually happens long before her body dies. That's the real tragedy.

A sure sign we are afraid of youthanasia is that women, especially those between the ages of thirty-five and fifty, account for almost half of all cosmetic procedures.[3] This speaks volumes.

Regain your footing

Step two in body acceptance as we age is to take back the ground we've given up. It's interesting that when we are young, we tend to worry about our weight, hips, legs, thighs, and stomach. You may be thinking, *Hmm, what's left?* Well, as we age, we shift our focus to eyes, hands, and fingers.[4] I guess this is because we have to see and feel our wrinkles before we can obsess over them!

I once heard an older person say aging is a state of mind that can be thought about too much if you don't use your time wisely. I believe that's true. The more we concentrate on what's lost versus what's gained, the unhappier we'll become. Perhaps it is time for a showdown with our mirrors. It will take a grassroots movement to stand in front of the looking glass and shout, "We're not going to take it anymore! Stop the madness! Long live the Dove girls!"

"Don't think of it as getting hot flashes. Think of it as your inner child playing with matches."

Before you dismiss me as some radical naturalist who's against makeup and anything cosmetic, that's not what I am saying. We have the choice to do things to improve or change our appearances. It's not a crime to have a Botox injection or use a chemical peel or have rhinoplasty. Go for it if that's what you want to do. I'm concerned more with the motivation behind those choices than with the procedures themselves.

What bothers me is the implication that if we *don't* pursue these things, we are lesser beings or in need of serious help. The thinking goes that an aging woman is broken and needs to be fixed. We might *feel* broken, but are we? Aging is a natural process in which the body breaks down. It brings aches and pains and a change in beauty, but it doesn't mean there is no beauty in it. It is just a different and perhaps more subtle form of beauty.

This is the normal course of life. We can mask the signs, but they still exist. So it's better to seek to adapt to the changes and concentrate on being healthy and fit instead of trying to look twenty-five again. This life is finite. Those of us who deny that fact view aging only as a sign of death, a move to finality. Yet in reality, the minute we are born, we begin the process of dying.

The sooner we realize that, the sooner we can get on with getting all we can out of the time we have left on this earth.

Exercise the power of choice

Step three should be empowering to you. We don't have to sit by silently or passively and be youthanized. We have options. Do something or do nothing; it's up to you. Just make it your choice, and let it be motivated by health and fitness and your personal well-being rather than some societal standard of beauty. Did you hear that? On this issue I am pro-choice. You can decide to do as little or as much "work" on your body as you feel comfortable doing. Just don't let the culture decide for you.

I loved it when actress Jamie Lee Curtis bared her real and natural body for *More* magazine back in 2002. If you missed it, she allowed herself to be photographed with no makeup and no hair styling, wearing a sports bra and biker shorts, and standing under bright lights. At the time, this was a daring and unthinkable move for any Hollywood actress.

But why not take that approach? I'm not saying you can't do the glamour photo shoot if you want to. Most of us like to play with makeup and new hairstyles. Just don't forget alternate views of what normal people look like as they age. And don't hide from the public when the wrinkles begin to appear.

Our bodies will change as we age. We may not like all the changes; I mean, who looks forward to an extra two to ten pounds with menopause? Who enjoys the thickening of their waist? But it happens! It's not the end of life as we know it unless we overvalue youth and undervalue maturity.

Wise up!

This brings me to my final suggestion. There is a huge blessing that can come only with age, if we'll let it. As we grow older, we gain maturity, wisdom, and perspective—all of which bring peace and purpose.

Maturity, though, is something to be worked for, something you attain. Aging will happen whether we work at it or not. Maturity won't happen unless we strive for it. Honestly, we need a balanced perspective. Otherwise we put undue pressure on ourselves, and the Lord knows we have enough other stuff to worry about.

Look, if you and I are going to make peace with our thighs, we've got to change our attitudes about aging. How we approach aging impacts how we feel about our bodies at any age. The more negative our attitudes, the worse we feel about our bodies. The more we fight the inevitable, the more exhausted we become.

Two things must happen: First, we have to change our ideas about aging and not feel compelled to cover up all the external changes. Second, we have to resist youthanasia in our culture and fight back.

We can be vital and attractive at any age. The next time you see an older woman, take time to look at her body. (Feel free to use me as an example next time you see me!) Study her and notice the changes that naturally occur. Then notice other things—her grace of movement, the brightness in her eyes, the spring in her step, the passion of her work. The more we look and notice, the more accepting we'll be, and the less aging will scare us.

"I've still got it, but nobody wants to see it."

Ladies, there is far more to our value than just our bodies, our shape, our skin, and our hair color. A quieted mind, the capacity to love deeply, spiritual maturity, passion, and wisdom are just a few benefits of aging. They're also part of its beauty. In fact, Proverbs 4:7–9 tells us to get wisdom above all else. It should be at the top of our list. Wisdom will make life glorious, garland it with grace, and festoon our days with beauty.

So here's your chance to make something special out of this season. Focus on who you are and why you are here, and engage in well-intended living. Invest in the younger generation and teach them what you know. Let's also reevaluate our attitudes toward aging and not just react to the programming of our culture and those who profit from our aging fears. Let's defy the youthanasia of our culture, acknowledging that making peace with our bodies requires us to age gracefully, one day at a time. Begin each day with a healthy respect for what your body has been through and accomplished. Thank God for what works and still functions. And remember, there is great purpose in your life as long as you live and breathe.

The choice is yours. Do you want to be remembered for looking ten years younger or for living a great life? By this point in the book, I hope you don't have to think on this very long. It's becoming more of a no-brainer for me with each passing day, and honestly, I like that. My story can be yours too.

For just one day, try living a great life rather than looking younger, and see if you don't feel better. Maybe that one day of refocused priorities and a happier you will turn into a week, and then a month, and then a year. If it does, you will have successfully conquered the Everest of the woman's world, youthanasia. And if you do reach the summit, write me so we can celebrate together!

PART THREE

Extreme Living

CHAPTER 14

When Peace Is Hard to Find

I began this book with the idea that body dissatisfaction is a universal issue for women. While it is normal to care about appearance, there is a point at which normal caring can turn obsessive and interfere with daily life.

❧❧

Karla is someone who has reached this point. At the age of twenty-seven, she is a newlywed who has a great job in public relations and is mom to a golden retriever puppy. Looking at Karla, you wouldn't notice anything out of the ordinary about her appearance. She is normal weight with brown hair, blue eyes, and a dimpled smile. Her body has good proportions, and her skin is smooth and clear. Karla appears to be a young, healthy adult who has everything going for her. Yet she spends most of her day entertaining thoughts of body hate.

The problem is that when Karla looks in the mirror, all she sees are her ears, and this bothers her to no end. Throughout the day Karla glances at her head and can't get past what she believes to be her incredible flaw. You or I would never single out Karla's ears as a negative part of her looks. But to Karla, they loom large. Compulsively, she touches them multiple times a day, constantly shoving them back toward her head.

Karla's discomfort with her ears is so intense that she has met with several plastic surgeons. Each one has said her ears are not that pronounced and don't need to be pinned back. Karla doesn't believe any of them and feels her protruding ears ruin her appearance. She can't stop thinking about how ugly she is, and consequently, she wears a hat whenever possible. Several of her coworkers have noticed this and wonder why. Rumor has it she is losing her hair from cancer treatments.

Thoughts about her appearance have recently affected her job in other ways. She is so bothered by her looks that she makes excuses to miss meetings, avoids her colleagues in the hall, and spends too much of the work day in the bathroom trying to cover her "problem." It's to the point that her boss has put her on probation for missing so many meetings, and her friends worry she is becoming isolated. This once-vibrant social butterfly is so self-conscious that she now spends her time hiding in her cubicle at work and refuses to go out at night.

Karla's husband is at a complete loss as to what to do. He repeatedly tells her that her ears look fine, that he doesn't even notice them under her hair. His frustration is growing because Karla will only make love now with the lights off. Even candlelight bothers her because she is convinced her husband will be sexually turned off by her physical imperfection. Karla refers to her ears as deformities and tries to hide them even in the bedroom.

None of this makes sense to Karla's husband, and no amount of his trying to convince her seems to make a difference. Karla continues to set up doctor appointments, searching for a plastic surgeon who will pin back her ears. Her job and marriage are suffering, yet she is oblivious to the true nature of her problem. Preoccupied with her appearance, Karla thinks of little else.

You might be thinking Karla has a simple case of vanity. That would be a mistake. When people are vain, they love themselves to a fault. Karla loathes her body and goes to great lengths to cover up and hide her imagined ugliness.

In talking with Karla, she recalls being called "Dumbo" one night while at a social get-together for work. Several people in the room were drinking too much, and one of the men approached Karla and tried to pick her up. When she rebuffed him, he made several gross remarks about her body. The one comment that stuck in Karla's brain was being called "Dumbo."

Karla was horrified that her coworker could be so rude, but she felt powerless to do anything about his insensitive remarks and sexual harassment. The entire evening felt out of control. The next morning, Karla dreaded getting ready for work. She was afraid to tell her husband what happened, thinking he would tell her boss or blame her for not reacting better. In recent months, Karla's reluctance to go to work has grown. Every morning, she has to talk herself into getting ready. And every morning, she finds a hat to cover her ears.

By now, you are very aware that cosmetic surgery is not a fix for any emotional problem. Karla's doctors know this to be true and picked up on her preoccupation. Recognizing the problem, they suggested counseling for Karla's heightened obsession, not surgery. The imagined ugliness that Karla sees is known as body dysmorphic disorder (BDD). It is a growing problem among men and women and is estimated to affect about 1–2 percent of the general population.[1] Like in Karla's life, the disorder for those with BDD becomes all-consuming and interferes with everyday living.

The anxious feelings Karla experiences are caused by thinking she has a flaw. In Karla's case, the flaw is her ears. Typically, people with BDD focus on parts of the face, their skin, thighs, stomach, breast size or shape, scars, thinning hair, or height, although any part of the body can become the target of extreme dislike and disparaging feelings. While each of us has some part of the body we'd like to change, BDD goes way beyond this normal dissatisfaction. The need to change or improve a body part becomes something that is thought about day and night. And when these thoughts get in the way of normal living, a person can become depressed and anxious. Some women even think about suicide and end up trying to take their own lives.

Like Karla, sufferers will try to hide the flaw or find ways to correct it. However, their efforts are fruitless. No amount of plastic surgery, exercise, or weightlifting will make them feel better, because the problem is on the inside, not the outside. It is the mind, not reality, that says a person is defective or flawed.

In many cases, BDD begins during adolescence or young adulthood with a single event like the one described above, where teasing or special attention to a person's appearance was involved. Many women who suffer with eating disorders also experience BDD. Sexual abuse and sexual harassment are also linked to the disorder. Researchers believe BDD shares the same core symptoms as obsessive compulsive disorder (OCD), but the obsessions and compulsions one has with BDD are related to appearances. Because of these similarities, treatment is similar.

Medications such as serotonin reuptake inhibitors (SSRIs) are frequently prescribed to help with anxious thoughts and compulsions. In addition, cognitive-behavioral treatments such as what I'll describe below are commonly used. And people must work on the social situations that make them feel anxious.

In Karla's case, the goal was to help her feel less anxious and change her thinking about her ears. First, she was asked to think about her ears, but not to look in the mirror or wear a hat. While working on her anxious thoughts, she was told not to ask anyone for reassurance concerning her appearance. In order to help Karla calm down while thinking in this scenario, body relaxation was taught.

Next, she was given several homework assignments. She was asked not to inspect her ears in the mirror, not to ask her husband how they looked, to stop calling plastic surgeons, and to stop wearing hats. In others words, she had to stop doing everything related to checking or hiding her perceived flaw and work on keeping her anxious feelings at bay.

Medication and relaxation skills helped her tremendously. In fact, medication was used first to help Karla feel less anxious so she could do the assignments. While Karla worked on the above homework, her husband was also given suggestions as to how to help her. He was asked not to react to her reassurance-asking questions and to resist commenting on how he didn't see any problems. His main job was to listen and offer support. Within four months, Karla stopped thinking about her ears every day and stopped wearing hats to work.

Not all people do as well as Karla did in such a short time. Some people have a very hard time giving up the belief that the perceived deformity is real. But if you are willing to trust a therapist, you can be helped. If you or someone you know struggles with this condition, contact a mental health therapist who has expertise in BDD, eating disorders, or OCD and get help now.

When the mirror lies

Sally was dying and we both knew it. The anorexia had ravaged her 5'2" frame. She sat quietly in my office looking more like a ten-year-old little girl than a twenty-one-year-old woman. At 72 pounds, she was facing her fifth hospitalization in a year.

Sally felt hopeless and abandoned. Her sunken eyes stared desperately at me. "I know I'm upsetting my family. I can't make myself eat, and I don't want to gain weight because I'm fat. I wish I could vanish or just disappear. Then I wouldn't upset anyone."

When Sally looks in the mirror, she sees a fat body, not a skeletal frame. Her feelings toward her body range from contempt to despair. Despite her emaciated appearance, her pursuit of thinness is unrelenting, and no amount of talk from caring loved ones convinces her otherwise.

Maureen is also consumed by the fear of getting fat. Every day she jumps on the scale, worried that she may have gained a pound or two. If the number moves up even the slightest bit, it ruins her day and she can think of nothing else. Feeling failed, she plans a food binge. Her personal life is in chaos. The man she dated was verbally abusive and her father phoned her drunk again last night. She feels out of control and rejected. "All I can think about is my next binge. Last night I ate an entire pizza, a pint of ice cream, and a bag of chips. I downed a two-liter bottle of Coke. Of course I felt sick and threw it all up. I feel so ashamed and worry all the time about getting fat. When I look in the mirror, I see a fat slob."

Maureen's weight is normal, but she suffers from bulimia, an eating disorder that involves a regular cycle of binging on food and then getting rid of it (purging). In Maureen's case, vomiting is the way she purges, but in the past she has used laxatives and diet pills to control weight gain. Maureen hates her body and feels fat all the time. Her unhealthy habits and relationship problems have landed her in an outpatient eating disorders group. She is trying to stop the destructive cycle of binge/purge behavior and find a way to accept her body.

Jordan faces serious health problems. Her joints ache, her blood pressure is too high, and she was just diagnosed with diabetes at the age of forty-four. I led her to the scale, where she weighed in at 305 pounds. "I keep gaining weight," she laments. "My latest diet, like all the others, isn't working. I don't know what else to do. It's like I can't stop eating. I know I'm hurting my body, but something overtakes me and I still eat. I think my boss is embarrassed about my size. He asked someone else to take clients out to lunch. He also told me I was passed over for a recent promotion."

Jordan hates her body as much as Maureen and Sally do, but she won't even look in the mirror. When she gets ready for work in the morning, she only looks at her face. In her mind, she isn't 305 pounds. She keeps telling herself that her binging isn't that bad . . . that she can get control over this tomorrow. When I ask her to talk about her body, she becomes very silent. "I don't like to think about my weight, and I avoid the scale because I don't want to know what the number is. I hate my size but try not to think about it or I'll get depressed."

When we see our bodies as enemies that won't conform to society's standards, and when our self-esteem is so low that we lose sight of our uniqueness, we are at risk for developing eating disorders. This is one of the reasons I have such concern for the media's narrowing definitions of femininity. The constant unrealistic images of the perfect body feed and reinforce our thoughts of being inadequate and failed. When these distortions become reality to us, we are in trouble.

The women mentioned above are three of approximately ten million girls and women who suffer from debilitating eating disorders. Of that number, 50,000 will die.[2] And while eating disorders are caused by a number of things, body image distortion is part of the problem that pushes many women over the edge.

You probably know someone who has or once had an eating disorder. If you live in a college dorm, you don't have to look far for evidence of the problem, because it is rampant on campuses. Or you might have picked up magazines with stories about Mary-Kate Olsen's fight with anorexia, Jane Fonda's history of bulimia, or Paula Abdul's binging. Many celebrities have come out of the eating closet and admitted to struggling with body image problems that have led to eating disorders. Because celebrities live in a fish bowl when it comes to appearance, it's easy to understand why they would be susceptible.

We've all been duped by a media strategy that vilifies fat people and convinces nine-year-old girls they need to diet. The media has partners—the food, diet, fashion, beauty, and healthcare industries. All dangle the thin carrot. We swallow it, even if it means possible death.

Something has to change. Someone needs to protest. And we all need to stop spending money on magical cures that promise the moon and deliver nothing. This is getting dangerous. People are being hurt.

Where the problem begins

Most eating disorders emerge at one of two points: around the time of puberty or when a young adult prepares to leave home. In the first case, as a child's body changes and she is faced with budding sexuality and pressure to become her own person, she may find herself obsessing on food as a way to control a life that feels out of control. Leaving home is another time of stress and transition. This usually begins in high school and continues as teens move out to attend college or enter the job market. The change in status requires independence and a growing sense of who you are. Body image is certainly a major focus during this stage of life and can become distorted with undue stress and relationship problems.

It used to be that only younger women were susceptible to developing eating disorders. This is no longer the case. Now, a growing number of women in their forties and fifties are seeking help for midlife eating disorders. Apparently, the stress of managing family, home, and career is taking a toll on middle-aged women.

In part, this new trend can be related to our obsession with youth and thinness. Forty-five-year-old women are told it's possible to look like twenty-five-year-olds. With fifty being the new thirty, and with cosmetic surgery going mainstream, and Botox block parties, and the growing number of personal trainers, as well as self-absorbed celebrities, it's a wonder any of us are sane when it comes to our bodies.

However, developing an eating disorder in midlife is more complex than just reacting to media. Years before menopause hits, fears related to aging may be realized. As I noted in the chapter on aging, midlife represents lost youth in our society. The fears of aging, changing bodies, launching children into the world, and marital breakups can trigger an obsession with food, weight, and exercise. If a person copes with life changes and losses through food and over-exercising, an eating disorder can develop.

Some women in midlife had eating disorders in their youth but were never really treated for them. The stresses of this season can trigger old habits, and the eating disorder can rear its ugly head again. Still others were diagnosed with an eating disorder in their youth but treatment was unsuccessful. When midlife stress and change is felt, the old eating disorder can reemerge.

And these midlife eating disorders create health problems—

some serious enough to lead to death. Osteoporosis, cardiac concerns, thinning hair, skin bruising, tooth decay, and gastrointestinal complaints are just a few dangers associated with self-starvation or binging and purging.

The pressure to look thin and beautiful is often what opens a door for serious body dissatisfaction. But there must be more to the picture than just body dissatisfaction or we would all be at risk. Other risk factors have to do with how we embrace the role of being a woman, negative family patterns such as avoiding conflict, individual personality factors, tendencies toward anxiety, depression, and other biologically based conditions, and experience around loss, abuse, and other trauma. As you can see, eating disorders are not caused by one single thing.

Because eating disorders are complex, professional counseling is needed to help free women from cultural prescriptions of beauty and body image. Other changes that need to be made include setting realistic expectations regarding performance at school and in the workplace, dealing better with relationships, handling conflict, letting go of perfection and people pleasing, releasing negative feelings, and stopping all-or-nothing thinking where one believes that things are either all bad or all good.

Family members are often frightened by the eating disorder because of the seriousness of related medical problems and because the person is misusing food. They can't understand the body distortions involved and spend a great deal of energy trying to convince a loved one she is thin enough or, in the case of those who binge only, that her weight is causing health problems.

Eating disorders require treatment by a mental health multidisciplinary team trained in this specialty. These disorders involve much more than food and weight. Early intervention is best because of the potential for serious medical problems, of which the extreme is death.

Simple starvation leads to anorexia nervosa; compulsive eating to binge eating disorder and obesity; and purging to bulimia nervosa. All three patterns share some things in common: intense fear of gaining weight, constant thoughts about food and eating, chronic dieting, poor body image, depression, and the need for approval by others.

The appendix at the end of this book includes the common signs of anorexia and bulimia. If you suspect you may be developing an eating disorder or know someone else at risk, find a licensed mental health provider who specializes in these disorders and begin treatment immediately. Your life may depend on it.

When an eating disorder or body dysmorphic disorder is involved, peace is hard to find. The mental, physical, and spiritual exhaustion that comes with these disorders can bring a sense of hopelessness. But don't despair or give in to the feeling of hopelessness. Help is available! People recover from these problems if they are treated and willing to accept help.

The key is to surrender the battle up front and allow those who are trained to help you. You must be willing to give up your false sense of control and learn to face life full force. Once you do, you too will be able to make peace with your thighs and the rest of your body.

Get on with Your Life

By now, I hope you love or at least like your thighs (or any other body part you have disliked or obsessed over) more than you did when you began this book. If this is still a leap of faith, then look at your thighs—or substitute your own body part—in the mirror and say something nice like, "Thighs, it's time you and I had a change of leg. Starting today, I'm ending the obsession, waving the white flag of surrender, and going to be kind to you guys. You might be a bit dimply and bigger than I would like, but you know, you are the only thighs I own, so let's make peace and be friends. I've got places to go, people to see, and things to do, and I don't want to waste another day worrying about your happiness." Pat them (don't pound them) on the sides and welcome them back to body acceptance.

Now to be fair, you can't just say a bunch of positive mumbo jumbo and hope to feel better about your life. Faith has to be followed up by action. You've got to apply what you've learned in this book. And of utmost importance is putting all the parts back into the whole.

Remember, you are body, soul, and spirit. So attend to your entire packaging. As you accept your body, flaws and all, you will need to engage your soul and spirit. The affirmations below, which are followed by actions, should help. Allow the Spirit in you to rise up and take control over your mind and body, because He alone can bring truth to your mind and peace to your soul.

In my physical body, I will

- exercise for toning, mood improvement, and health reasons, not to build the perfect body.
- refuse to use cosmetic surgery to fix my inner life.
- be careful with my words, knowing they have the power to tear down or build up.
- keep physical attraction in its proper perspective and not make it the most important part of my relationships.
- do what I can do to be healthy and look good, but not cross the line.

In my mind, I will

- think of myself as a whole person, not just parts.
- stop negative and degrading thoughts and replace them with caring, loving, and positive statements about my body.
- fight against youthanasia and embrace the normal process of aging, focusing on the positive benefits.
- understand that distortion is a natural part of the human experience and continue to renew my mind and spirit with God.
- not covet my neighbor's body part or body.
- relinquish the false sense of control I think I have over life and work on my reactions to life—the one thing I can control.

- not believe the myth that my body is broken and needs fixing.
- not buy into cultural prescriptions of beauty.
- refocus my life on values that endure and have meaning.
- examine reasons for wanting to change or modify my body and make sure I am not making changes for the wrong reasons.
- understand the biology of desire and have realistic expectations.

In my emotions, I will

- confront emotional pain and life difficulties and not use my body as a distraction or false way to control life.
- stop comparing myself to other people.
- find a Jan for my life.
- feel sexy and confident no matter how imperfect my physical body is.
- improve my mood by accepting compliments and asserting myself.
- remove myself from toxic relationships and environments.
- seek professional help if I cross the line and can't find peace.

In my spirit, I will

- come to God just as I am, understanding His unconditional acceptance and love for me.
- forgive the people who have hurt me and not allow them to have power over me.
- respect God and do what He tells me to do.
- stop listening to the opinions of others and learn what God has to say about me.
- accept my uniqueness and individuality as being God-given.

I'd like us to think of this book as a wake-up call. Even though we can laugh and cry at our crazy lives, most of us need to make changes in our thoughts, emotions, relationships, and the culture with which we surround ourselves.

Take inventory concerning your body. Examine your value system. Be conscious of what society tells you about who you are and what you are supposed to be. Above all, listen to the One who made you, who loves you without condition, and who wants you whole and well. It is possible to reclaim and redefine our bodies as ours. Today, let's make peace with our thighs and rejoice!

I thank you, High God—you're breathtaking!
Body and soul, I am marvelously made!
I worship in adoration—what a creation![1]

The Signs[1]

Signs of anorexia

- Weight loss and refusal to gain to normal weight (15 percent below an acceptable weight is in the clinical range for anorexia)
- Intense fear of becoming fat or gaining weight
- Body image disturbance
- Loss of menstruation
- Wearing baggy clothing to cover body form
- Cutting up food in tiny pieces; moving food around the plate instead of eating it
- Weighing food and obsessing on calories
- Excessive exercise
- Preoccupation with food and dieting
- Physical and medical symptoms related to weight loss (dry skin and hair, cold hands and feet, weakness, consti-

pation, digestive problems, infections, metabolic distur-
bances, stress fractures, osteoporosis, heart problems, mild
anemia, swollen joints)

- Weighing multiple times a day
- Foods are discussed as "good" or "bad"
- Anxiety when eating with others
- Fatigue
- Feelings of worthlessness and hopelessness
- Signs of depression—loss of interest in things that were previously cared about, poor concentration, irritability, agitation, restlessness, withdrawal, sleep problems, suicidal thoughts

Signs of bulimia

- Binging and purging occurs at least twice a week for a three-month period
- Obsession with body weight and shape
- Body image distortion
- Feeling out of control
- Fear about gaining weight
- Purging to compensate for binges (vomiting, laxative abuse, diet pills, etc.)
- Medical problems such as the wearing away of enamel on teeth from acid when vomiting, scarring on the backs of hands from having fingers in the mouth to vomit, inflamed esophagus, swollen cheek glands, irregular menstrual periods, dehydration, and electrolyte imbalance
- Diminished interest in sex
- Feelings of depression

Signs of binge eating

- Lack of control over eating
- Consuming a large amount of food or calories in a short time

- Eating until feeling uncomfortably full
- Eating alone because of being embarrassed over how much is eaten
- Feeling disgusted, guilty, or depressed over what was eaten
- Body shape and weight concerns
- On average, happens two days a week over a six-month period
- Chronic dieting
- Weight gain
- Belief that problems are due to weight and that food is the only friend

Resources

Body Dysmorphic Disorder (BDD)

For more information on BDD, including what it is, how a person sees herself, and what is needed to help, please see the fact sheet at www.4women.gov/bodyimage/BDD.cfm?doPrint=yes.

Books

Alcorn, Nancy. *Mercy for Eating Disorders: True Stories of Hope and Real Answers for Healing and Freedom*. Franklin, TN: Providence House Publishers, 2003.

Arterburn, Stephen and Ginger Garrett. *Lose It for Life for Teens: The Spiritual, Emotional, and Physical Solution*. Brentwood, TN: Integrity Publishers, 2005.

Arterburn, Stephen and Linda Mintle. *Lose It for Life: The Total Solution for Permanent Weight Loss*. Brentwood, TN: Integrity Publishers, 2004.

Bevere, Lisa. *You Are Not What You Weigh:Escaping the Lie and Living the Truth*. Lake Mary, FL: Creation House, 1998.

Mintle, Linda. *Breaking Free from Anorexia and Bulimia: How to*

Find Healing from Destructive Eating Disorders. Lake Mary, FL: Charisma House, 2002.

Mintle, Linda. *Overweight Kids.* Brentwood, TN: Integrity Publishers, 2005.

Eating Disorders Organizations

National Eating Disorders Association (NEDA)
603 Stewart Street, Suite 803
Seattle, WA 98101-1264
Web site: www.nationaleatingdisorders.org
Phone: (800) 931-2237

National Association of Anorexia Nervosa and Associated Disorders (ANAD)
P.O. Box 7
Highland Park, IL 60035
Web site: www.anad.org
Phone: (847) 831-3438

To learn more about Dr. Linda Mintle, visit her Web site:

www.drlindahelps.com.

"Glad you found me. Pull up a chair, get comfortable and stay awhile. Although this isn't a therapy site, it is a place to find helpful tips, advice, and information about relationships, emotional problems, and the tough issues of life. Learn more about how to get unstuck from life's problems and live in victory versus defeat."

E-mail is welcome: drlindahelps@yahoo.com

Endnotes

Get off the Scales

1. Kate Fox, "Mirror, mirror: A summary of research findings on body image," Social Issues Research Centre, 1997. Retrieved online Nov. 14, 2005, from http://www.sirc.org/publik/mirror.html.

1. Thighs and Sighs of the Times

1. 1 Corinthians 13:12.

2. The Hair Is Always Blonder on the Other Side

1. Holly VanScoy, "Redheads Are a Tough Knockout in Surgery," Health Scout News, ABC News.com, 2002. Retrieved online Fall 2005, from http://www.redandproud.com/Red%20Academy%20Tough%20In%20Surgery.htm.

4. Breasts—What Would Barbie Do? (WWBD)

1. Quote from the documentary *Body Image: The Quest for Perfection*, produced by Kelly Briley, 2000. Retrieved online from www.bodyimagesite.com.

2. "The Barbie Doll." Retrieved online Oct. 19, 2005, from http://www.ideafinder.com/history/inventions/story081.htm.

3. Retrieved online Feb. 23, 2006, from http://en.wikipedia.org/wiki/Barbies.

4. Judith Duffy, "Barbie's figure 'gives young girls a desire to have

a thinner body,'" *Sunday Herald* online, June 12, 2005. Retrieved online Oct. 19, 2005, from http://www.sundayherald.com/50249.

5. "Life in Plastic," Economist.com, Dec. 19, 2002. Retrieved online Oct. 20, 2005, from http://www.economist.com/people/displayStory .cfm?story_id=1487595.

6. Ibid.

7. Ingeborg Majer O'Sickey, "Barbie Magazine and the Aesthetic Commodification of Girls' Bodies," *On Fashion*. Ed. Shari Benstock and Suzanne Ferriss. (New Brunswick, NJ: Rutgers University Press, 1994) 21–40.

8. "Life in Plastic," Economist.com, Dec. 19, 2002.

9. V.G. Koste, *Dramatic Play in Childhood: Rehearsal for Life* (Portsmouth, NH: Heinemann, 1995).

10. Quote from the documentary *Body Image: The Quest for Perfection*, produced by Kelly Briley, 2000. Retrieved online from www.body imagesite.com.

11. "Mother Defends Teenager's Breast Operation," BBC News, Jan. 4, 2001. Retrieved online from http://news.bbc.co.uk/1/hi/health/ 1100471.stm.

12. Ibid.

13. Catherine Solyom, "How young is too young? Breast implant debate continues," July 24, 2004. Retrieved online from http:// canoe.talksurgery.com/consumer/new/new00000054_2.html.

14. Michael Olding, M.D. and Diana Zuckerman, Ph.D., "Cosmetic surgery and teens," *Washington Post* Health Feature, Oct. 26, 2004. Retrieved online Oct. 20, 2005, from http://www.washingtonpost .com/wp-dyn/articles/A63931-2004Oct26.html.

15. Brinton LA; Lubin JH; Burich, MC; Colton T; Hoover, RN; "Mortality Among Augmentation Mammoplasty Patients," *Epidemiology* (Vol. 12, 2001), 321–26.

16. Ibid.

17. Catherine Refern, "Teenagers and Cosmetic Surgery," The F word: Contemporary UK Feminism. Retrieved online Feb. 24, 2006, from http://www.thefword.org.uk/features/2001/04/teenagers_and _cosmetic_surgery.

18. Merril Haseen, "The biggest boob." Retrieved online Oct. 19, 2005, from http://www.theanswerbank.co.uk/Article185.html.

19. *That Body Image Thing: Young Women Speak Out*, edited by Sara Torres. Retrieved online Oct. 24, 2005, from The Canadian Women's

Health Network, http://www.cwhn.ca/network-reseau/2-4/body image.html.

20. Ruth Handler with Jacqueline Shannon, *Dream Doll: the Ruth Handler Story* (Stamford, CT: Longmeadow Press, 1994), 212–13. Retrieved online Oct. 20, 2005, from "Barbie Meets Breast Cancer" by Ellen Leopold, http://www.bcaction.org/Pages/SearchablePages/2005Newsletters/Newsletter087C.html.

5. Stomach Aches

1. D. Garner, "Survey says: Body image poll results," *Psychology Today*, Feb. 1997. Retrieved online Nov. 15, 2005, from http://www.psychologytoday.com/articles/pto-19970201-000023.html.

2. Mary Ann Mayo and Dr. Joseph Mayo, *The Menopause Manager*, Revell. Grand Rapids, Michigan: Revell, 1998), 178.

3. Ibid.

4. T. Pope-Parker, "Belly Fat May Be the Body's Way of Coping with Stress," *The Wall Street Journal*, July 19, 2005. Retrieved online Nov. 4, 2005, from http://www.azcentral.com/health/diet/articles/0719 wsj-belly-fat19-ON.html.

5. I appear frequently on this television show, which airs daily at 10:00 EST on ABC Family (cable).

6. Abs and sit-up information was copied from the UABHS Office of Medical Publication in conjunction with UAB Health Systems physicians. *Dear Doctors: Muscles (Toning)*, Nov. 3, 2005. Retrieved online Nov. 3, 2005, from http://www.health.uab.edu/show.asp?durki=67577&site=734&return=18687.

7. Ibid.

8. Excerpts taken from Mote Marine Laboratory Newsletter article, "How to Deflate a Fish." Retrieved online Oct. 30, 2005, from http://www.catchandreleasefound.org/deflate.htm.

9. Medical Encyclopedia. Retrieved online Nov. 4, 2005, from http://www.nlm.nih.gov/medlineplus/ency/article/002978.htm#Risks.

10. H. Bruch, *Conversations with Anorexics* (New York: Basic Books, Inc., 1988).

11. Oswald Chambers, Jan. 22, "Am I looking to God?" *My Utmost From His Highest* (Grand Rapids, MI: Discovery House Publishers, 1935).

12. Romans 12:2.

13. Retrieved online Nov. 22, 2005 from http://www.wordreference.com/definition/attention.

14. Ephesians 4:15–18.
15. Psalm 51:10 (NAS).

6. A Pain in the Butt

1. "Anatomy of the Gluteus Maximus." Retrieved online Nov. 16, 2005, from http://www.fitstep.com/Advanced/Anatomy/Glutes.htm.
2. Retrieved online Oct. 30, 2005, from http://www.cosmetic surgery.com/research/cosmetic-surgery/Buttock-Implants.
3. "Nike Steers Advertising Toward Big Butts and Thunder Thighs," Aug. 16, 2005. Retrieved online Nov. 17, 2005, from http://playahata .com/hatablog/?p=787.
4. R. Morgan Griffin, "Fighting Cellulite: 'Jean' Therapy to Creams," July 12, 2004. Retrieved online from http://www.webmd.com/content/ Article/90/100731.htm?pagenumber=1.
5. L. Kravitz, "Cellulite: Everything You Want to Know and More." Retrieved online Nov. 16, 2005, from http://www.drlenkravitz.com/ Articles/cellulite.html.
6. P. Francis, "Anti-Cellulite Jeans Hit the Market." Retrieved online Nov. 19, 2005, from http://www.klastv.com/Global/story.asp?S= 1884974.
7. R. Morgan Griffin, "Fighting Cellulite: 'Jean' Therapy to Creams," July 12, 2004.
8. Ibid.
9. "Getting Rid of Cellulite." Retrieved online Nov. 18, 2005, from http://www.medicinenet.com/script/main/art.asp?articlekey=51220.

7. An About Face

1. A. Rankman, "Obsessed with Beauty: The Rush to Cosmetic Surgery," Oct. 7, 2005. Retrieved online Nov. 26, 2005 from http:// www.aphroditewomenshealth.com/news/cosmetic_surgery.shtml.
2. Song of Solomon 1:2 (NAS).
3. William Shakespeare, *Romeo and Juliet*. Act I, Scene V.
4. Ibid., Act V, Scene III.
5. C. Rowland, "Fuller Lips: How Lip Enhancement Works." Retrieved online Nov. 26, 2005, from http://ezinearticles.com/?Fuller -Lips—How-Lip-Enhancement-Works&id=94073.
6. Ibid.
7. "Babies Recognize Face Structure Before Body Structure," Blackwell Publishing, Jan. 1, 2005. Retrieved online Nov. 26, 2005 from http://www.sciencedaily.com/releases/2005/01/050104114623.htm.

8. Ibid.

9. Ibid.

10. Ibid.

11. Viktor Frankl, *Man's Search for Meaning: An Introduction to Logotherapy* (New York: Washington Square Press, 1969), 104.

12. Isaiah 46:5; 40:25–26.

13. Isaiah 53:2–3.

14. Ephesians 1:4–5.

15. 1 John 3:1.

16. Romans 8:16.

17. 2 Corinthians 3:18.

9. You and Me and Body Make Three

1. Proverbs 18:21 (NIV).

2. "Christopher Reeve Dies at 52," CNN News. Retrieved online Dec. 6, 2005, from http://edition.cnn.com/2004/SHOWBIZ/Movies/10/11/obit.reeve.

10. Dates and Mates

1. S. Parker, M. Nichter, N. Vuckovic, C. Sims, C. Ritenbaugh, "Body Image and Weight Concerns among African American and White Adolescent Females: Differences that Make a Difference," *Human Organization* (Vol. 54, No. 2, Summer 1995), 103–14.

2. C. Pyant, and B. Yanico, "Relationship of Racial Identity and Gender-role Attitudes to Black Women's Psychological Well-being," *Journal of Counseling Psychology* (Vol. 38, 1991), 315–22.

3. M. R. Cunningham, A. R. Roberts, A. P. Barbee, P. B. Druen, and C. Wu, "Their ideas of beauty are, on the whole, the same as ours: Consistency and variability in the cross-cultural perception of female physical attractiveness," *Journal of Personality and Social Psychology*, (Vol. 68, 1995), 261–79.

4. D. J. Bowen, N. Tmoyasu, and A. Cauce. "The Triple Threat: A Discussion of Gender, Class, and Race Differences in Weight," *Women and Health* (Vol. 17, No. 4, 1991), 124–43.

5. "Determinants of Female Beauty," Newsdial.com. Retrieved online Dec. 7, 2005, from http://www.newsdial.com/relationships/dating/female-beauty.html.

6. P. C. Regan, "Sexual outcasts: The perceived impact of body weight and gender on sexuality," *Journal of Applied Social Psychology* (Vol. 26, 1996), 1803–15.

7. "Determinants of Male Physical Attractiveness," Newsdial.com. Retrieved online Dec. 7, 2005, from http://www.newsdial.com/relation ships/dating/male-attractiveness.html.

8. N. Li, J. Bailey, D. Kenrick, and J. Linsenmeier, "The necessities and luxuries of mate preferences: Testing the tradeoffs," *Journal of Personality and Social Psychology* (Vol. 82, 2002), 947–55.

9. "She Knows: Cads or Dads." Retrieved online Dec. 7, 2005, from http://sheknows.com/about/look/1802.htm.

11. Victoria's Secrets

1. T. Smith, "American Sexual Behavior: Trends, Socio-Demographic Differences, and Risk Behavior," National Opinion Research Center, University of Chicago, GSS Topical Report No. 25 (Dec. 1998). Retrieved online Dec. 13, 2005, from http://cloud9.norc.uchicago.edu/dlib/t-25.htm.

2. Retrieved online from http://www.ptm.org/01PT/JulAug/revenge.htm.

3. D. M. Ackard, A. Kearney-Cooke, and C. B. Peterson, "Effect of body image and self-image on women's sexual behaviors," *International Journal of Eating Disorders* (Vol. 28, No. 4, 2000), 422–29.

4. "Body Image and Identity." Retrieved online Dec. 7, 2005, from http://www.sexualityandu.ca/eng/health/SOW/bodyimage.cfm.

5. 1 Corinthians 6:17, adapted.

6. M. P. Koss, "Hidden Rape: Sexual Aggression and Victimization in the National Sample of Students in Higher Education," *Violence in Dating Relationships: Emerging Social Issues,* eds. M.A. Pirog-Good & J. E. Stets (New York, NY: Praeger, 1988), 145–68.

7. D. Curtis, "Perspectives on Acquaintance Rape," The academy of experts in traumatic stress, 1997. Retrieved online Dec. 13, 2005, from http://www.aaets.org/arts/art13.htm.

8. R. Bergen, "Marital Rape." Applied research Forum, National Electronics Network on Violence Against Women, March, 1999. Retrieved online Dec. 13, 2005, from http://www.vawnet.org/Domestic Violence/Research/VAWnetDocs/AR_mrape.pdf.

9. Ibid.
10. Ibid.
11. Ibid.
12. Ibid.
13. Ibid.

14. "Adult Survivors of Incest." Retrieved online Dec. 13, 2005, from http://www.icasa.org/uploads/adult_survivors_of_incest.pdf.

15. D. Russell, *The Secret Trauma: Incest in the Lives of Girls and Women* (New York: Basic Books, Inc. Publishers, 1986).

16. C. Courtois, *Healing the Incest Wound: Adult Survivors in Therapy* (New York: W.W. Norton & Company, 1988).

17. Ibid.

12. Not in the Mood

1. "Body Image, not Menopause, Lowers Desire," *Journal of Sex Research* (Dec. 19, 2005). Retrieved online Dec. 28, 2005 from http://www.lifescript.com/channels/well_being/News_Bites/body_image_not_menopause_lowers_desire.asp.

2. M. Hitti, "How to Help a Woman's Body Image," WebMD Medical News. Source: Courtney Fea, MS, Kansas State University. American Psychological Association 17th Annual Convention, Los Angeles, May 26–29, 2005. News release, Kansas State University. Retrieved online Dec. 29, 2005, from http://www.webmd.com/content/Article/106/108235.htm?pagenumber=1.

3. Delores King, "Exercise Seen Boosting Children's Brain Function," *Boston Globe*, Nov. 9, 1999. Retrieved online Nov. 13, 2005. http://www.pelinks4u.org/archives/interdisciplinary/070201.htm.

4. Andrew Lane, Andrew Jackson, and Peter Terry, "Preferred Modality Influences on Exercise-Induced Mood Changes," *Journal of Sports Science and Medicine* (Vol. 4) 195–200. Retrieved online Nov. 13, 2005, from http://www.jssm.org/vol4/n2/13/v4n2-13pdf.pdf.

5. Loui Tucker, "Dance as Therapy." Retrieved online Nov. 12, 2005, from http://www.louitucker.com/dance/DanceAsTherapy.htm.

6. Andrew Lane, Andrew Jackson, and Peter Terry, "Preferred Modality Influences on Exercise-Induced Mood Changes," *Journal of Sports Science and Medicine* (Vol. 4).

13. Youthanasia

1. "Body Image: Looking For, and Liking, the Real You." Retrieved online Dec. 22, 2005, from http://www.mothernature.com/Library/Bookshelf/Books/44/12.cfm.

2. Ibid.

3. Ibid.

4. "Body Image and Midlife." Retrieved online Jan. 2, 2006, from http://www.rwh.org.au/wellwomens/whic.cfm?doc_id=2886.

14. When Peace Is Hard to Find

1. Statistics taken from an interview with J. Kevin Thompson, author of *Exacting Beauty: Theory, Assessment, and Treatment of Body Image Disturbance.* Retrieved online Jan. 3, 2006, from http://www.athealth.com/Consumer/disorders/BDDInterview.html.

2. C. Hartline, "Dying to Fit In—Literally! Learning to Love Our Bodies and Ourselves," International Eating Disorder Referral Organization, Body Image. Statistics retrieved online Jan. 6, 2006 from http://www.edreferral.com/body_image.htm.

Get on with Your Life

1. Psalm 139:14.

Appendix: The Signs

1. This list is based loosely on the Diagnostic and Statistical Manual of Mental Disorders (DSM-IV), along with other material from my personal clinical experience of more than twenty years.

Look for these other great titles
by Dr. Linda Mintle

What You Say and Do Now Will Affect Your Children for a Lifetime!

A staggering 30 percent of American youngsters —twice as many as 20 years ago—are overweight or on their way to becoming so. Nearly 20 percent of those diagnosed as obese are under the age of five.

In *Overweight Kids*, Dr. Mintle has assembled positive, practical, preventive and inspirational guidelines to help parents find spiritual and behavioral solutions to help their children: develop a healthy body image; learn to make good food choices and have healthy eating habits; create a fun, physically active lifestyle; avoid the pitfalls that lead to overeating while developing self-control; and deal with teasing and negative comments.

Filled with stories of triumphs, hope and encouragement, along with plenty of practical advice, *Overweight Kids* contains parenting strategies that will help your child grow into a healthy weight.

Available wherever books are sold • ISBN 1-59145-283-X

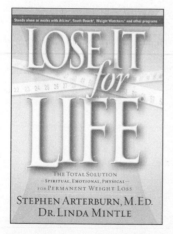

Tired of That Old Yo-Yo Weight Loss/Weight Gain Cycle? Lose It for Life!

Most weight-loss plans will help you drop a few pounds, but for how long? You deserve better. You deserve *Lose It for Life*, a uniquely balanced program that deals with the physical, emotional and even spiritual elements that lead to permanent weight loss.

Even if you have already experienced some success on another weight-loss program, this book will give you the information and motivation you need to achieve a permanent "state of weightlessness," which is *the* secret to lasting results.

Lose It for Life was developed by best-selling author and radio personality Stephen Arterburn who lost 60 pounds 20 years ago and has kept it off. In this revolutionary book, he and Dr. Linda Mintle, who is known for her clinical work regarding weight issues, will help you accomplish what you desire most: permanent results.

Available wherever books are sold • ISBN 1-59145-245-7

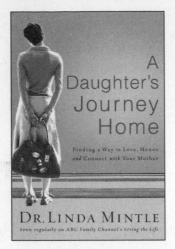